# Lecture Notes in Computer Science 12992

More information about this subseries at https://link.springer.com/bookseries/7409

Ruifeng Xu · Cheng Cai ·
Liang-Jie Zhang (Eds.)

# Cognitive Computing – ICCC 2021

5th International Conference
Held as Part of the Services Conference Federation, SCF 2021
Virtual Event, December 10–14, 2021
Proceedings

*Editors*
Ruifeng Xu (ID)
Harbin Institute of Technology
Shenzhen, China

Cheng Cai
Shanghai Dianji University
Shanghai, China

Liang-Jie Zhang (ID)
Kingdee International Software
Group Co., Ltd.
Shenzhen, China

ISSN 0302-9743        ISSN 1611-3349   (electronic)
Lecture Notes in Computer Science
ISBN 978-3-030-96418-4        ISBN 978-3-030-96419-1   (eBook)
https://doi.org/10.1007/978-3-030-96419-1

LNCS Sublibrary: SL3 – Information Systems and Applications, incl. Internet/Web, and HCI

This Springer imprint is published by the registered company Springer Nature Switzerland AG
The registered company address is: Gewerbestrasse 11, 6330 Cham, Switzerland

# Preface

The International Conference on Cognitive Computing (ICCC) was created to cover all aspects of Sensing Intelligence (SI) as a Service (SIaaS). Cognitive computing is a sensing-driven computing (SDC) scheme that explores and integrates intelligence from all types of senses in various scenarios and solution contexts. It is well beyond traditional human senses, which comprise the four major senses (sight, smell, hearing, and taste) located in specific parts of the body as well as the sense of touch located all over the body.

ICCC 2021 is a member of Services Conference Federation (SCF). SCF 2021 featured the following 10 collocated service-oriented sister conferences: the International Conference on Web Services (ICWS 2021), the International Conference on Cloud Computing (CLOUD 2021), the International Conference on Services Computing (SCC 2021), the International Congress on Big Data (BigData 2021), the International Conference on AI and Mobile Services (AIMS 2021), the World Congress on Services (SERVICES 2021), the International Conference on Internet of Things (ICIOT 2021), the International Conference on Cognitive Computing (ICCC 2021), the International Conference on Edge Computing (EDGE 2021), and the International Conference on Blockchain (ICBC 2021).

This volume presents the accepted papers for ICCC 2021, held as a fully virtual conference during December 10–14, 2021. The major topics of ICCC 2021 included, but not limited to, cognitive computing technologies and infrastructure, cognitive computing applications, sensing intelligence, cognitive analysis, mobile services, cognitive computing on smart home, and cognitive computing on smart city.

We accepted eight papers, comprising five full papers and three short papers. Each paper was reviewed by three independent members of the ICCC 2021 Program Committee. We are pleased to thank the authors whose submissions and participation made this conference possible. We also want to express our thanks to the Program Committee members for their dedication in helping to organize the conference and reviewing the submissions. We look forward to your future contributions as volunteers, authors, and conference participants in the fast-growing worldwide services innovations community.

December 2021

Ruifeng Xu
Cheng Cai
Liang-Jie Zhang

# Organization

## ICCC 2021 Program Chairs

| | |
|---|---|
| Ruifeng Xu | Harbin Institute of Technology, China |
| Cheng Cai | Northwest A&F University, China |

## Services Conference Federation (SCF 2021)

### General Chairs

| | |
|---|---|
| Wu Chou | Essenlix Corporation, USA |
| Calton Pu | Georgia Tech, USA |
| Dimitrios Georgakopoulos | Swinburne University of Technology, Australia |

### Program Chairs

| | |
|---|---|
| Liang-Jie Zhang | Kingdee International Software Group Co., Ltd., China |
| Ali Arsanjani | Amazon Web Services, USA |

### Industry Track Chairs

| | |
|---|---|
| Awel Dico | Etihad Airways, UAE |
| Rajesh Subramanyan | Amazon Web Services, USA |
| Siva Kantamneni | Deloitte Consulting, USA |

### CFO

| | |
|---|---|
| Min Luo | Georgia Tech, USA |

## Industry Exhibit and International Affairs Chair

| | |
|---|---|
| Zhixiong Chen | Mercy College, USA |

## Operations Committee

| | |
|---|---|
| Jing Zeng | China Gridcom Co., Ltd., China |
| Yishuang Ning | Tsinghua University, China |
| Sheng He | Tsinghua University, China |

## Steering Committee

| | |
|---|---|
| Calton Pu (Co-chair) | Georgia Tech, USA |
| Liang-Jie Zhang (Co-chair) | Kingdee International Software Group Co., Ltd., China |

## ICCC 2021 Program Committee

| | |
|---|---|
| Luca Cagliero | Politecnico di Torino, Italy |
| M. Emre Gursoy | Koc University, Turkey |
| Meng Han | Kennesaw State University, USA |
| Nagarajan Kandasamy | Drexel University, USA |
| Carson Leung | University of Manitoba, Canada |
| Supratik Mukhopadhyay | Louisiana State University, USA |
| Roberto Natella | Federico II University of Naples, Italy |
| Rui André Oliveira | University of Lisbon, Portugal |

# Conference Sponsor–Services Society

The Services Society (S2) is a non-profit professional organization that has been created to promote worldwide research and technical collaboration in services innovations among academia and industrial professionals. Its members are volunteers from industry and academia with common interests. S2 is registered in the USA as a "501(c) organization", which means that it is an American tax-exempt nonprofit organization. S2 collaborates with other professional organizations to sponsor or co-sponsor conferences and to promote an effective services curriculum in colleges and universities. The S2 initiates and promotes a "Services University" program worldwide to bridge the gap between industrial needs and university instruction.

The Services Sector has account for 79.5% of the GDP of United States in 2016. The world's most services oriented economy, with services sectors accounting for more than 90% of GDP. The Services Society has formed 10 Special Interest Groups (SIGs) to support technology and domain specific professional activities.

- Special Interest Group on Web Services (SIG-WS)
- Special Interest Group on Services Computing (SIG-SC)
- Special Interest Group on Services Industry (SIG-SI)
- Special Interest Group on Big Data (SIG-BD)
- Special Interest Group on Cloud Computing (SIG-CLOUD)
- Special Interest Group on Artificial Intelligence (SIG-AI)
- Special Interest Group on Edge Computing (SIG-EC)
- Special Interest Group on Cognitive Computing (SIG-CC)
- Special Interest Group on Blockchain (SIG-BC)
- Special Interest Group on Internet of Things (SIG-IOT)

# About Services Conference Federation (SCF)

As the founding member of the Services Conference Federation (SCF), the first International Conference on Web Services (ICWS) was held in June 2003 in Las Vegas, USA. Meanwhile, the First International Conference on Web Services - Europe 2003 (ICWS-Europe'03) was held in Germany in Oct, 2003. ICWS-Europe'03 is an extended event of the 2003 International Conference on Web Services (ICWS 2003) in Europe. In 2004, ICWS-Europe was changed to the European Conference on Web Services (ECOWS), which was held at Erfurt, Germany. SCF 2020 was held successfully. To celebrate its 19-year-old birthday, SCF 2021 was held virtually over the Internet on December 10–14, 2021.

In the past 18 years, ICWS community has been expanded from Web engineering innovations to scientific research for the whole services industry. The service delivery platforms have been expanded to mobile platforms, Internet of Things, cloud computing, and edge computing. The services ecosystem is gradually enabled, value added, and intelligence embedded through enabling technologies such as big data, artificial intelligence, and cognitive computing. In the coming years, all the transactions with multiple parties involved will be transformed to blockchain.

Based on the technology trends and best practices in the field, SCF will continue serving as the conference umbrella's code name for all services-related conferences. SCF 2021 defines the future of New ABCDE (AI, Blockchain, Cloud, big Data, Everything is connected), which enable IOT and enter the 5G for Services Era. SCF 2021's 10 co-located theme topic conferences all center around "services", while each focusing on exploring different themes (web-based services, cloud-based services, Big Data-based services, services innovation lifecycle, AI-driven ubiquitous services, blockchain driven trust service-ecosystems, industry-specific services and applications, and emerging service-oriented technologies). SCF includes 10 service-oriented conferences: ICWS, CLOUD, SCC, BigData Congress, AIMS, SERVICES, ICIOT, EDGE, ICCC and ICBC. The SCF 2021 members are listed as follows:

[1] The 2021 International Conference on Web Services (ICWS 2021, http://icws. org/) is the flagship theme-topic conference for Web-based services, featuring Web services modeling, development, publishing, discovery, composition, testing, adaptation, delivery, as well as the latest API standards.

[2] The 2021 International Conference on Cloud Computing (CLOUD 2021, http:// thecloudcomputing.org/) is the flagship theme-topic conference for modeling, developing, publishing, monitoring, managing, delivering XaaS (everything as a service) in the context of various types of cloud environments.

[3] The 2021 International Conference on Big Data (BigData 2021, http:// bigdatacongress.org/) is the emerging theme-topic conference for the scientific and engineering innovations of big data.

[4] The 2021 International Conference on Services Computing (SCC 2021, http:// thescc.org/) is the flagship theme-topic conference for services innovation

lifecycle that includes enterprise modeling, business consulting, solution creation, services orchestration, services optimization, services management, services marketing, business process integration and management.

[5] The 2021 International Conference on AI & Mobile Services (AIMS 2021, http://ai1000.org/) is the emerging theme-topic conference for the science and technology of artificial intelligence, and the development, publication, discovery, orchestration, invocation, testing, delivery, and certification of AI-enabled services and mobile applications.

[6] The 2021 World Congress on Services (SERVICES 2021, http://servicescongress.org/) puts its focus on emerging service-oriented technologies and the industry-specific services and solutions.

[7] The 2021 International Conference on Cognitive Computing (ICCC 2021, http://thecognitivecomputing.org/) puts its focus on the Sensing Intelligence (SI) as a Service (SIaaS) that makes system listen, speak, see, smell, taste, understand, interact, and walk in the context of scientific research and engineering solutions.

[8] The 2021 International Conference on Internet of Things (ICIOT 2021, http://iciot.org/) puts its focus on the creation of Internet of Things technologies and development of IOT services.

[9] The 2021 International Conference on Edge Computing (EDGE 2021, http://theedgecomputing.org/) puts its focus on the state of the art and practice of edge computing including but not limited to localized resource sharing, connections with the cloud, and 5G devices and applications.

[10] The 2021 International Conference on Blockchain (ICBC 2021, http://blockchain1000.org/) concentrates on blockchain-based services and enabling technologies.

Some highlights of SCF 2021 are shown below:

– **Bigger Platform:** The 10 collocated conferences (SCF 2021) get sponsorship from the Services Society which is the world-leading not-for-profits organization (501 c(3)) dedicated for serving more than 30,000 worldwide Services Computing researchers and practitioners. Bigger platform means bigger opportunities to all volunteers, authors and participants. Meanwhile, Springer provides sponsorship to best paper awards and other professional activities. All the 10 conference proceedings of SCF 2021 have been published by Springer and indexed in ISI Conference Proceedings Citation Index (included in Web of Science), Engineering Index EI (Compendex and Inspec databases), DBLP, Google Scholar, IO-Port, MathSciNet, Scopus, and ZBlMath.

– **Brighter Future:** While celebrating 2021 version of ICWS, SCF 2021 highlights the Fourth International Conference on Blockchain (ICBC 2021) to build the fundamental infrastructure for enabling secure and trusted services ecosystems. It will also lead our community members to create their own brighter future.

– **Better Model:** SCF 2021 continues to leverage the invented Conference Blockchain Model (CBM) to innovate the organizing practices for all the 10 theme conferences.

# Contents

# Research Track

# An Annotated Speech Corpus of Rare Dialect for Recognition—Take Dali Dialect as an Example

Tian Huang, Dongqi Yang, Wanyun Qin, Shubo Zhang, Binyang Li, and Yan Li[✉]

University of International Relations, Beijing, China
liyan@uir.edu.cn

**Abstract.** Nowadays, the widespread use of Automatic Speech Recognition technology, aided by AI products, has made people's lives easier. Despite significant progress in Mandarin recognition in Chinese, a number of rare dialects remain unrecognized due to a lack of the corresponding speech corpus. In this paper, we propose a method for creating a rare dialect speech corpus using daily spoken words as recording content. Following the labeling of all dialect audios, a dialect speech corpus with complete information, including speech, text, and labeling, is established. Experimenting with a Dali dialect speech corpus of 2400 audios demonstrates the efficacy of the proposed method. Finally, the verification of annotation consistency using the Kappa value clearly improves the quality of the Dali dialect speech corpus.

**Keywords:** Dialect speech corpus annotation · Rare dialect · Automatic Speech Recognition

## 1 Introduction

Automatic Speech Recognition is the process of converting human voice signals into text or instructions. This is a critical area of research in voice signal processing and a subfield of pattern recognition. In recent years, Automatic Speech Recognition has grown by leaps and bounds and piqued the interest of academic and business circles due to its wide applicability and commercial potential. The more mature applications are currently based on voice input control systems, e.g., Siri. This system can recognize the request, command, or question in the speech and respond appropriately, making human-machine communication straightforward. Furthermore, Automatic Speech Recognition could also be used to translate spoken language, allowing voice input from one language to be converted into voice output from another language for multilingual communication [1].

Automatic Speech Recognition requires the specific speech corpus as the training data. Current corpora are always oriented on popular languages like English, French, Chinese, etc. The lack of speech corpus in rare languages and dialects limits the scope of Automatic Speech Recognition applications. For example, during the COVID-19 time

R. Xu et al. (Eds.): ICCC 2021, LNCS 12992, pp. 3–13, 2022.
https://doi.org/10.1007/978-3-030-96419-1_1

in 2020, numerous medical staff from other regions arrived at Wuhan for assistance, but many of them were unable to communicate with local patients, particularly the elderly. The Wuhan dialect and Mandarin, on the other hand, have a major linguistic gap. Fortunately, iFlytek gathered dialects in the Wuhan area, established a related speech corpus, and applied Automatic Speech Recognition technology to solve the Wuhan doctors-patients communication challenge. However, China has a large geographical region and numerous language variations. The existing dialect speech corpus is far from enough to cover all Chinese dialects. Therefore, it is imminent to find an efficient way to build a dialect corpus.

Despite the fact that several organizations some companies have built a quite comprehensive dialect speech corpora, these corpora have not been made available, and academics are still unable to access relevant data. Simultaneously, these companies established a speech corpus centered on the province as a unit. However, even within the same province, dialects vary to variable degrees, resulting in a considerable number of errors in the Automatic Speech Recognition process. Taking Yunnan dialect as an example, Table 1 illustrates that there are various problems in picking Yunnan dialect utilizing Iflytek's speech dictation feature.

**Table 1.**  An example of incorrect Automatic Speech Recognition.

| Original text | English interpretation | Iflytek | English interpretation |
|---|---|---|---|
| 明天去哪点闲? | Where to play tomorrow? | 明天去哪点想? | where to think tomorrow? |

The problem in Table 1 is not only with the speech corpus established by those companies but also with the dialect corpora established by other researchers, which have inadequate data or are not practical, resulting in substantial inaccuracies in the real application of the speech corpus. As a result, an acceptable dialect-based speech corpus that can effectively increase the quantity of dialect corpora is required.

In this paper, we proposed a modified method for systematically creating dialect corpora. We use our own distinct annotation rule in this method, which applies to the annotation of speech in dialects from various locations. It is quite adaptable and can be tailored to the characteristics of many dialects. This work created a series of representative dialect speech databases with a clear structure and complete data while establishing the specific dialect corpora. Its construction process, information architecture, and implementation experience make it a dialect speech corpus creation method with a high reference value for other dialects when creating comparable corpora.

We use the Dali dialect speech corpus (DDSC) as an example to demonstrate the efficacy of our method. The texts on DDSC in this experiment are all in colloquial language. The annotation principle was developed in conjunction with Chinese pronunciation standards and the speaking characteristics of the Dali people. This principle is strictly followed by the annotation of DDSC. Experimenting with a 2400 audio Dali dialect speech corpus demonstrates the efficacy of the proposed method. Finally, using the Kappa value to verify annotation consistency clearly improves the quality of the Dali dialect speech corpus.

The remaining manuscript is structured as follows: Sect. 2 contains a brief overview of related work. In Sect. 3, we introduce our speech corpus's construction method. All experiments on DDSC and their results are described in Sect. 4, and our conclusions are finally summarized in Sect. 5.

## 2 Related Work

We mainly explore and study the related work from two aspects: Popular Speech Corpus, and Rare Speech Corpus.

### 2.1 Popular Speech Corpus

As China's Official Common Language, Mandarin is the reference standard for the construction of other language speech corpora in China. Therefore, when constructing a new speech corpus, it is necessary to refer to the Mandarin speech corpus based on preserving the language's unique features, with the feature index and audio text aligned in both directions. Therefore, the construction of the Mandarin standard speech corpus has become more mature and comprehensive. In 2003, [2] put forward the RASC863, which is a standardized collation and exploration of Mandarin influenced by dialects. These include the four major dialects of Mandarin: Shanghai, Guangzhou, Chongqing, and Xiamen. The data set includes the natural spoken language part, the reading part of commonly used spoken sentences, and dialect vocabulary. In the oral part, 160 topics are set up, and the speaker chooses one by random. Then they tell you the relevant content for 4–5 min. The reading corpus is a total of 2,200 sentences with balanced pronunciation and 600 commonly spoken sentences. There are 200 speakers for each dialect point, for a total of 800 speakers. In 2007, [3] proposed TH-CoSS, which is mainly oriented to speech synthesis research. The speech corpus is mainly selected from news, including Mandarin male/female voice reading statements, exclamations, questions, sentence length of 5–25 syllables. In addition, the speech corpus also recorded a certain number of neutral tones, rhotic accents, and ascending monosyllables. The annotation of speech data includes Chinese characters, Pinyin with the tone, syllable boundaries, and prosodic boundaries. [4] proposed an open-source Mandarin Chinese speech database (AISHELL-ASR0009-OS1) in 2017, which contains 179 h of audio files recorded by 400 speakers from different regions of China. The recorded text covers the fields of finance and economics, science and technology, sports, entertainment, and so on. The data set has been checked and annotated by professional speech proofreaders, and the accuracy of the text is over 95%. In 2018, [5] proposed a larger 1000-h Mandarin Corpus, Aishell-2, based on Aishell-1, which is the largest available speech corpus. The speech corpus is widely used in Automatic Speech Recognition, model training, and machine translation projects.

In addition to Mandarin, many organizations or universities around the world have created speech corpora of other foreign languages. The British Academic Spoke English (BASE) project took place at the Universities of Warwick and Reading between 2000–2005 [6]. After that, BASE Plus was also launched. There is also a project to establish a speech corpus for Scottish, which has some similarities and differences with English. The Scottish Corpus of Texts & Speech (SCOTS) has been online since November 2004, and, after several updates and additions, has reached a total of nearly 4.6 million words of text, with audio recordings to accompany many of the spoken texts [7]. A sister resource, the Corpus of Modern Scottish Writing, was launched in 2010, and now comprises 5.4 million words of written text with accompanying images. They have created large electronic databases of written and spoken texts for the languages of Scotland.

## 2.2  Rare Speech Corpus

The local language is referred to as a dialect because it differs from Mandarin in some ways. When compared to the Mandarin speech corpus, the Chinese dialect speech corpus is still severely lacking. Currently, almost all public Chinese speech corpus sets in China are concentrated on Mandarin. There are just a handful of publicly accessible dialect speech corpora. Simultaneously, several large companies, such as Iflytek and Baidu AI, have created relatively complete dialect speech corpora, however, these dialect speech corpora have not been made public. Despite the fact that researchers in certain studies created a fairly limited speech corpus on their own. However, some of the self-constructed speech corpora, such as the author's in [9], have relatively little data. The author gathered a total of 2,244 isolated word recording files from the recordings of four volunteers to create a speech corpus. Because it is only made up of the voices and other data of four volunteers, its speech corpus is not entirely representative of the region. In the other section, for example, [9] used widely distributed local films and TV works, such as "Wang Baochang's biography" and "Happiness Harrow's ear". The completed speech corpus contains 1,490 speech pieces of data. This method, however, may not be suited for all dialects. Furthermore, certain widely circulated local film or audio from the past, and their context and daily language habits, are not always in sync with the present. The actual application will have certain errors. The accuracy of Automatic Speech Recognition cannot be compared to Mandarin in terms of the present dialect speech corpus. More speech corpora are required. The regional components of the dialect speech corpus are further decreased to increase the accuracy of Automatic Speech Recognition.

China is wealthy in multilingual resources. Aside from the Chinese-related speech corpus, development on a minority national speech corpus is also underway. Many minority corpora have been used in a variety of circumstances. There are two types of minority languages: those with their characters and those that rely on Chinese characters. The method for creating a national speech corpus with its own characters is currently the same as that for creating an English speech corpus. However, due to a scarcity of characters, they must continue to rely on Chinese characters since carriers of national language library creation methods are still few.

## 3  Method of Speech Corpus Construction

For the construction of dialect speech corpus, our main work consists of four parts: Data Selection, Audio Recording and Processing, Annotation Schema Design, and Audio Annotation. Our workflow is shown in the following Fig. 1.

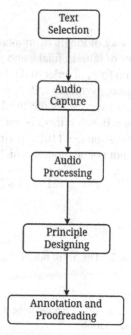

**Fig. 1.** The workflow of our work.

## 3.1 Data Selection

The proper text for the creation of the dialect speech corpus must first be chosen. We must consider the application situations of dialects while selecting texts and avoid poetry, written language, and so on. We should primarily use daily language as the text to improve the usage of the final speech corpus. Because the Chinese dialect is based on Mandarin, when selecting the text, the publicly accessible Mandarin text can be utilized, followed by the necessary everyday conversations.

## 3.2 Audio Recording and Processing

We must first determine the audio specifications and audio file naming rules during the audio recording and processing process. When selecting the proper recording equipment and environment, we must limit the influence of external elements on the final data, according to the audio specifications. Due to the regional nature of dialects, the best way to obtain audio is to go to the local area and choose suitable volunteers for audio recording. We make every effort to choose volunteers who will reside in the location where the dialect is spoken for an extended period to reduce the interference of other languages. At the same time, the volunteer's age, gender, family background, social status, and so on can cover the larger the scope, the better. These volunteers are in good health, have no illnesses associated with language expression, and can assure precise and clear speech. Finally, the processing approach used for the common speech corpus should be employed to assure the availability of the final data after processing the gathered audio.

### 3.3   Annotation Schema Design

For the annotation, we refer to the way of Pinyin to annotate Mandarin and incorporated improvements. Annotation consists of initials, finals, and tones. And we have made particular adjustments in the annotation form in order to deal with the machine recognition. To represent tones, we used the number symbols 1, 2, 3, 4, 5, where 1 represents the first tone, 2 represents the second tone, 3 represents the third tone, 4 represents the fourth tone, and 5 represents the light tone. Besides, there is another improvement. According to the Scheme of Chinese Phonetic Alphabet [10], Pinyin may make up a total of 802 articulatory combinations that do not contain tones, which are (Table 2):

$$(IN + IE) * FI + VO + RH + NG - DU = (21 + 2) * 35 + 9 + 1 + 3 - 16 = 802.$$
$$(1)$$

**Table 2.** The list of notations.

| IN | IE | FI | VO | RH | NG | DU |
|---|---|---|---|---|---|---|
| Initials | Consonants Sound the Same as Vowels | Finals | The pronunciation beginning with the three vowels: *a, e, o* | Rhotic accent | Syllables pronounced by *ang, eng, ong* | Duplicates caused by the repeated writing of vowel U |

Although these 802 combinations will not be used completely in Mandarin or certain dialects, they will cover the pronunciation of Mandarin and the majority of dialects. The principle is expected to apply to additional dialects with specific adjustments.

### 3.4   Audio Annotation

The annotation method follows the specifications and processes of the annotation principle. In terms of annotation people, it differs from general speech corpus annotations. Because dialect characters and speech contrast are based on Mandarin, selectors must be fluent in Mandarin and understand Chinese Pinyin use norms. For annotation formatting, a common "text-tone" format is utilized to assure the generality of the annotation application.

Different annotation versions of the same audio are compared to assure annotation accuracy, and consistency is detected using Kappa values. The differences between versions are then modified and confirmed to obtain the final uniform annotation standard.

## 4   The Experiment of Dali Dialect Speech Corpus

For DDSC, we used the method of Sect. 3 to complete the construction of the corpus.

## 4.1 Experimental Configuration

First, we prepare the necessary equipment for the speech corpus-building process, such as recording equipment such as a RODE NT-USB Mini microphone, a Dell computer, and a USB flash drive for data storage. Volunteers were chosen at the same time. We selected 20 volunteers who had resided in Dali, Yunnan, for a long period. The ratio of male to female volunteers is 1:1, and they are between 20–50 years old.

Following that, we select the King-ASR-L-009 corpus, which covers everyday language and has practical value. Each text has 120 sentences. King-ASR-main L-009's body covers a broad range of themes, including daily greetings, holiday blessings, and promotional slogans. We initially looked for open-source Chinese speech data sets such as THCHS30, AISHELL, and Speechocean. Because Dali is a popular tourist destination, two-thirds of the population is Bai. Furthermore, some people are unable to speak in Mandarin. With the widespread adoption of compulsory education policies and the rapid expansion of higher education, locals prefer to use Mandarin in more formal settings. In contrast, dialect is more like an auxiliary language. Therefore, spoken sentences are more valuable in the development of the Dali dialect speech corpus. The THCHS30 and Aichelle data sets, on the other hand, are larger but less practical value (Table 3).

**Table 3.** Statistics on DDCS.

| Sentence # | Word # | Average length of sentences | Repetition rate |
| --- | --- | --- | --- |
| 2,400 | 31,063 | 12.94 | 1.81% |

Finally, the recorded audio is named as follows: the first eight digits of the file name indicate the date of recording, the ninth to tenth digits identify the day's recorder, and the eleventh to twelfth digits indicate the date of recording. The text's final three digits indicate that the audio represents the first few phrases of the text. This naming pattern guarantees that pertinent audio information is quickly identified during use.

## 4.2 Experimental Results

Each participant recorded 120 sounds at a sampling rate of 48000 Hz and a bit rate of 16 bits. If the volunteers become stuck during the recording process, their pronunciation is unclear, or other issues arise, they must record again. To avoid audio quality loss caused by external influences, the complete recording procedure is carried out in a calm interior setting at the same time. Finally, after several recordings, 2,400 first audio recordings were collected.

The recorded audio is processed and saved as a standard format, i.e., a wav file, while the original audio naming is preserved. We picked easy-to-use audio processing software and set up a noise reduction system to handle the collected audio. To achieve the goal of audio preprocessing, such as blanking, muting, and noise reduction. For example, if the audio level drops too low during processing, the audio gain is boosted to restore normalcy. Second, if the audio has a pause of more than 0.3 s at the start, finish, or midway part, the blank mute will be removed based on the audio track. To do preliminary noise reduction on the recorded audio, we utilize the automated noise reduction option in the software's audio effect. We examine the noise reduction effect of the audio once again using the effective control and make minor manual modifications to various parameter values. We select Export Audio > Export Audio in.wav format once the audio has been processed. Finally, the audio processing is completed, and its size is altered from 208 KB to 1622 KB as a result of the processing.

The table below gives instances of the Dali dialect and Putonghua annotation based on the concept and features of the Dali dialect (Table 4).

**Table 4.** Dialect pronunciation and Mandarin pronunciation.

| Text | English Interpretation | Dali Dialect | Mandarin |
|------|------------------------|--------------|----------|
| 摘草莓 | Picking strawberries | zhei1cao1mei4 | zhai1cao3mei2 |
| 城墙 | City wall | ceng4qiang4 | cheng2qiang2 |
| 可靠 | Reliable | kou1kao3 | ke3kao4 |
| 老师 | Teacher | lao1si2 | lao3shi1 |
| 学习 | Study | xiu4xi4 | xue2xi2 |

In the initial labeling stage, we assigned 20 people to label them based on the existing numbers of 2,400 voice dates, on the premise of adhering to the above-mentioned labeling standards and methods. These relevant people all meet the following requirements: standard Mandarin pronunciation, a complete understanding of the Scheme of the Chinese Phonetic Alphabet speech specifications, and the ability to clearly distinguish error-prone content such as front and back nasal sounds, curled tongue, and five tones.

In order to effectively assure annotation correctness and eliminate standard inconsistency caused by mistakes and other variables. The 2400 audios acquired are organized into groups to be annotated by various personnel. The annotation versions of various persons are distinguished. In this process, there should be at least two versions of the effective annotation result of the same audio.

There are presently 2,400 pieces of voice data, corresponding text data, and preliminary annotation data.

### 4.3 Correction of Experimental Results

We use the kappa value to verify the consistency of annotations, which is also widely used in medical examinations, imaging medicine, and other research work consistency [11].

The verification process ensures that at least two annotation versions of the same audio are available. The Kappa value is used to evaluate the consistency of several tag versions. Statistically, we find a kappa value of 0.68. The variations between all versions should be documented and validated. These distinctions were contrasted and analyzed by choosing 20 Dali people who represented Dali dialects. Determine the annotation version depending on the individual scenario and the practicality of the Dali dialect. All annotations that differ from one another must be changed and rectified. Finally, we arrive at the best version of each remark, bringing the overall kappa up to 0.81.

Following audio annotation, a collection of complete annotation results matching to the text corpus's words and sentences is first acquired. As can be observed from the results, although Dali dialect and Mandarin are closely linked, there is a distinct difference between the two in terms of more complex transformation rules. Three common modifications of the Dali dialect compared to Mandarin are listed in the three tables below. The last table contains several terms that are entirely unique to the dialect and have no relation to the comparable expressions in Mandarin. The pronunciation of the entire term is also changed, with different tones, initials, finals, and even length. During the annotating process, it was discovered that the pinyin of certain words seemed undefined in the Chinese Phonetic Alphabet, but could be articulated using its rules (Table 5).

**Table 5.** Examples of results. The table on the left shows words with only pitch changes. The middle shows words whose initials and vowels have also changed in addition to pitch. The right shows the words have changed in all three parts.

| Text | Dali Dialect | Mandarin | Text | Dali Dialect | Mandarin | Text | Dali Dialect | Mandarin |
|---|---|---|---|---|---|---|---|---|
| 白天 | bai4tian2 | bai2tian1 | 日出 | ri4cu1 | ri4chu1 | 怎么 | za1guo3 | zen3me4 |
| 公园 | gong2yuan4 | gong1yuan2 | 餐厅 | cang1ting1 | can1ting1 | 这么 | za1guo3 | zhe4me4 |
| 喜欢 | xi1huan3 | xi3huan1 | 权衡 | quan4hen4 | quan2heng2 | 和 | da1 | he2 |
| 媳妇 | xi4fu5 | xi2fu4 | 感冒药 | gan1mao3you4 | gan3mao4yao4 | 去 | ke4 | qu4 |
| 满足感 | man1zu1gan1 | man3zu1gan3 | 老师 | lao1si3 | lao3shi1 | 干啥呢 | gao1shen4me4 | gan4sha2ne5 |

# 5 Conclusion

In this paper, we propose a method for creating a sparse speech corpus and use DDSC as an example to demonstrate its applicability. This speech corpus is based on the King-ASR-L-009 dataset from the SpeechOcean company, which has 2,400 voices. Every word in the complete dataset, which contains 2,400 phrases and 32,283 words, was annotated. We compare the annotation results with Pinyin. The distinctions between the Dali dialect and Mandarin are then summarized in terms of tone, Pinyin composition, and expression. It can be used as a reference in the construction of corpora in Dali's surrounding areas, such as Tengchong and Kunming.

In the future, we will apply DDSC to speech recognition and apply the database establishment principles to other dialects.

**Acknowledgements.** This work was partially supported by the National Natural Science Foundation of China (Grant number: 61976066), Beijing Natural Science Foundation (Grant number: 4212031), the Fundamental Research Fund for the Central Universities (Grant numbers: 3262020T20, 3262021T23), and Research Funds for NSD Construction, University of International Relations (Grant numbers: 2019GA43, 2019GA35).

# References

1. Karmakar, P., Teng, S.W., Lu, G.: Thank you for Attention: a survey on Attention-based Artificial Neural Networks for Automatic Speech Recognition (2021)
2. Li, A., Wang, T., Yin, Z.: RASC-863 an annotated speech corpus with 4 accents. In: NCMMSC7 (2003)
3. Cai, L., Cui, D., Cai, R.: TH-CoSS, a mandarin speech corpus for TTS. J. Chin. Inf. Process. **21**(2), 94–99 (2007)
4. Bu, H., et al.: Aishell-1: an open-source mandarin speech corpus and a speech recognition baseline. In: 2017 20th Conference of the Oriental Chapter of the International Coordinating Committee on Speech Databases and Speech I/O Systems and Assessment (O-COCOSDA). IEEE (2017)
5. Du, J., Na, X., Liu, X., et al.: Aishell-2: transforming mandarin research into industrial scale. arXiv preprint arXiv:1808.10583 (2018)
6. Dang, T., Webb, S.: The lexical profile of academic spoken English. Engl. Specif. Purp. **33**, 66–76 (2014)
7. Douglas, F.M.: The Scottish corpus of texts and speech: problems of corpus design. Literary Linguist. Comput. **18**, 23–37 (2003)
8. Yu, X.: Speech Recognition of Hainan Dialect Based on Deep Learning. Hainan University (2020)
9. Fu, J., Li, Y., Tao, W., Luo, J., Li, W.: Chengdu dialect recognition based on convolutional neural network. J. China West Normal Univ. (Nat. Sci.) **41**(04), 440–444 (2020)
10. Chou, E.: Current Tasks of Word Reform (Excerpt). Editor of the Character Reform Press. Formulation and Application of Scheme of Chinese Phonetic Alphabet—Collected Works Commemorating the 25th Anniversary of the Publication of Scheme of Chinese Phonetic Alphabet. Character Reform Press, Beijing (1983)
11. Guo, Y., Guo, W., Qin, Y., He, Q., Zhang, X., Wu, C.: Consistency test based on Kappa coefficient and its software implementation. China Health Stat. **33**(01), 169–170+174 (2016)
12. Huang, S., Wang, D.: Review of corpus research in China. J. Inf. Resour. Manag. **11**(03), 4–17+87 (2021)
13. Sri, G.: Construction of "Modern Mongolian Corpus Management Platform". Inner Mongolia University, Huhehot (2010)
14. Shu, Q., Vuritu, N.: Construction of Chinese-Mongolian Bilingual corpus for EBMT system. Inner Mongolia Soc. Sci. **1**, 140–144 (2006)
15. Bilikz. The Experimental Study on the Corpus Based Word Frequency Statistics of Modern Uighur Language. Xinjiang University, Urumqi (2003)

16. Gao, D., Sonam-Sangmu: Research on the type number of samples in the construction of large tibetan language balanced corpus. J. Tibet Univ. **28**(1), 54–58 (2013)
17. Shen, Q.: The choice of sampling rate and quantization bit depth in audio work. Audio Technol. (02), 54–55+60 (2013)

# Contrastive Learning for Multiple Models in One Supernet

Sean Xu[1], Yihui Li[1], Yice Zhang[1], Ruifeng Xu[1(✉)], Jianxin Li[2], Guozhong Shi[2], and Feiran Hu[2]

[1] Joint Lab of HITSZ-CMS, Harbin Institute of Technology (Shenzhen), Shenzhen, China
{19s051059,20s051013}@stu.hit.edu.cn, xuruifeng@hit.edu.cn
[2] China Merchants Securities Co., Ltd., Shenzhen, China
{lijx,shiguozhong,hufeiran}@cmschina.com.cn

**Abstract.** Autonomous Machine Learning (AML) alludes to a learning framework having an adaptable trademark to develop the construction and boundaries on the fly. It is empowered by the way that AMLs means to adjust among stability and plasticity of a learning system. At present, deep learning-based unsupervised learning is another intriguing issue in the field of Autonomous Machine Learning, among which multi-architecture optimization is of extraordinary trouble in this research area. At the point when the current calculations face multi-intellectual model issues, it frequently sets aside a great deal of effort to ceaselessly set diverse looking through functions of different boundaries to look for the ideal model. In this work, we propose a novel technique for multi-model contrastive learning, which can get diverse unsupervised learning structures that are fit for deploying under different budgets, through a single shot super-network. Experiments reveal that our algorithm can boost the performance of the existing methods.

**Keywords:** Neural Architecture Search · Unsupervised learning · Model compression

## 1 Introduction

Autonomous Machine Learning (AML) refers to a learning system having flexible characteristics to evolve both its network structure and parameters on the fly. It is fit for starting its taking in measure without any preparation with/without a predefined network structure while its information base is built up continuously. AML is based upon two key standards: one-pass learning methodology and self-evolving network structure. The previous one mirrors a circumstance where a data point is straightforwardly disposed of once learned to guarantee limited memory and computational burdens while the latter lies in the self-reconfiguration aptitude of AML where its network size can increment or lessen with varying information circulations.

© Springer Nature Switzerland AG 2022
R. Xu et al. (Eds.): ICCC 2021, LNCS 12992, pp. 14–23, 2022.
https://doi.org/10.1007/978-3-030-96419-1_2

Currently, deep learning-based unsupervised learning is a new hot topic in the field of Autonomous Machine Learning. With the rapid development of industrial applications in various areas, massive data has been accumulated. Processing and analyzing the data content to obtain valuable information has become a key task. More and more deep learning and neural network models have been applied to industrial applications. However, the design and verification of a suitable and excellent deep learning-based cognitive automation model for the application of industrial applications often require a lot of human labor, such as selection algorithm, super parameter adjustment, iterative modeling, and model evaluation. Therefore, if there is a way that can automatically find the right solution to the current unsupervised problem, it can effectively save the artificial labor of scientists and liberate the creativity of researchers.

Contrast learning is a type of self-supervised learning, which means that one does not rely on annotated data and has to learn knowledge from unannotated images on their own. In general, self-supervision in the image domain can be divided into two types: generative self-supervised learning and discriminative self-supervised learning. VAE [1] and GAN [2] are two typical types of generative self-supervised learning methods, i.e. they require a model to reconstruct an image or a part of an image, which is a relatively difficult task requiring pixel-level reconstruction, and the intermediate image encoding must contain a lot of detailed information. Contrastive learning, on the other hand, is typically discriminative self-supervised learning, which is a less difficult task than generative self-supervised learning.

Neural Architecture Search (NAS) is a new research direction and one of the hot topics in automated machine learning (autoML). By designing a cost-effective search method, the neural network structure with strong generalization ability and hardware friendliness can be obtained automatically, which saves a lot of human costs. Its deployment and use are more suitable for industrial promotion and application. NAS is designed to solve the problem that designing deep learning networks heavily relying on the profound knowledge of experts, aiming to achieve competitive performance while automating the neural network architecture designing process. For some tasks like image recognition, NAS has yielded very promising results. NAS can serve as a useful tool to help us with the issue of Contrast learning.

There is a keen hypothesis that should be considered in the unsupervised learning process. Encoder $f$ should belong to a function family $\mathbf{F}$ of functions $f$ within which $f$ can map pictures uniformly to higher spaces. We assume that in a family of functions, a representation can be efficiently learned from another representation learned by comparison mapped with another model.

In our study, we employ two key techniques, the first being contrast learning between sub-models and the second being a contrast learning loss function that combines its contrast learning with a maximum model distillation contrast.

In this paper, we propose a method based on One-Shot Neural Architecture Search to realize the aim of training multi-models by a super network.

- By introducing a OneShot superNet structure, representations produced by different structures can be compared with each other for contrastive learning.
- we propose a novel type of multi-model contrastive learning loss for learning the for different network structures efficiently.

Experimental results demonstrate that our method is effective for getting multiple unsupervised training models under different computation budgets.

## 2 Related Work

### 2.1 Unsupervised Learning

The main idea of contrastive learning, which has been recently popularized for self-supervised representation learning, is to draw in the positive sample pairs and rebuff the negative sample pairs. Siamese networks were widely used in many simple and effective research methods of contrastive learning.

In practice, contrastive learning methods benefit from a large number of negative samples, which can be maintained in a memory bank. In a Siamese network, MoCo [3] maintains a queue of negative samples and transforms one branch into a momentum encoder to further develop consistency of the queue. SimCLR [4] directly straightforwardly utilizes negative examples coexisting in the current batch, and it requires a large batch size to function well.

BYOL [5], which is a Siamese network in which one branch is a momentum encoder, straightforwardly predicts the yield of one view from another view. It is speculated that the momentum encoder is important for BYOL to avoid collapsing, and it reports failure results if removing the momentum encoder.

However, empirical research in SimSiam [6] challenges the need for the momentum encoder for preventing collapse. They find that the stop-gradient operation is critical. This discovery can be obscured with the usage of a momentum encoder, which is always accompanied by a stop-gradient method. While the moving-average behavior may improve accuracy with a suitable momentum coefficient, their experiments show that it is not directly related to preventing collapse. The training protocol is shown in Fig. 1.

### 2.2 Neural Architecture Search

NAS is designed to solve the problem of automatically designing deep learning networks, aiming to achieve competitive performance. For some tasks like image recognition, NAS has yielded very promising results.

The main methods of neural architecture search can be divided into three categories, using reinforcement learning and evolutionary learning, as well as other algorithmic methods. In terms of reinforcement learning, Zoph et al. [7] used RNN as the controller to transform the sequence generated by RNN into a model and learn neural architectures through reinforcement learning. In terms of evolutionary algorithms, Liu et al. [8] and Real et al. [9] designed two search spaces for evolutionary algorithms, and used genetic algorithms to search neural

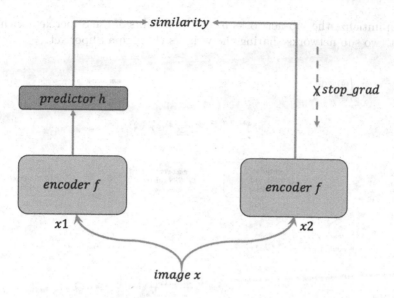

**Fig. 1.** SimSiam training protocol

architectures in these search spaces. In other algorithms, Liu et al. [10] proposed to use differentiable neural architecture search (DNAS) to discover hardware-aware efficient Neural Networks. However, training the network to convergence requires huge resources, many techniques have emerged to accelerate the search speed of neural networks. When it comes to the acceleration of the NAS process, some approaches were proved to be effective, such as parameter sharing, network morphism, and one-shot architecture search.

# 3    Method

## 3.1    Multi-model Contrastive Learning

There is a keen hypothesis that should be considered in the unsupervised learning process. Encoder $f$ should belong to a function family $\mathbf{F}$ of functions $f$ within which $f$ can map pictures uniformly to higher spaces.

We assume that in a family of functions, a representation can be efficiently learned from another representation learned by comparison mapped with another model.

In our study, we employ two key techniques, the first being contrast learning between sub-models and the second being a contrast learning loss function that combines its contrast learning with a maximum model distillation contrast.

In the unsupervised training phase, one forward pass is made for two different augmentations of a single image, and two different sub-networks are used to process the different augmentation to obtain two different representations. During the training process, we randomly sample two different networks separately and then initialize the sub-networks using the weights of the SuperNet, with the different two sub-networks sharing the weights through a SuperNet.

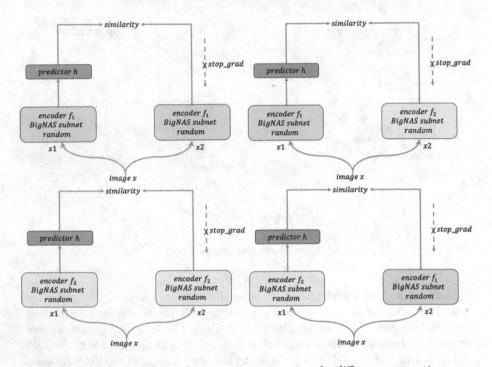

**Fig. 2.** Submodels Contrastive Learning manner, using the different contrastive representations produced by different submodels.

At the same time, due to the existence of two different augmentation branches in contrast learning, for example, the two sampled networks will be computed separately for two different augmentations, and two different representations will be obtained separately. A cross-over process will be performed to compute the contrast learning loss for these four representations to obtain the final contrast learning loss (as shown in the Fig. 2).

Comparing sub-models against each other for the entire search space can lead to excessive complexity in training. Based on this consideration, we used a maximum model representation pair sampling for the process of sub-model learning from each other.

That is, in the combined "contrast learning" loss function, we consider the contrast loss between the submodels and the representation obtained by searching the maximal model, as well as the contrast loss of the representation obtained by the submodels themselves (as shown in Fig. 3).

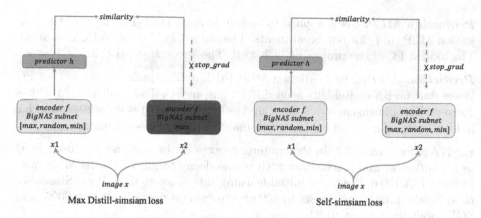

**Fig. 3.** Max-Distil constrastive loss and self constrastive loss

## 3.2 Coarse-to-Fine Architecture Selection

After training a single-stage model, one requirement is to select the best network design of different resource budgets. Even though obtaining the precision of a child model is modest, the quantity of architecture candidates is extremely huge.

To address this issue, we referred to BigNAS [13], propose a coarse-to-fine technique where we first attempt to track down a rough skeleton of promising network candidates in general, and afterward sample multiple fine-grained variations around each skeleton architecture of interest.

In particular, in the coarse-grained phase, we characterize a restricted input resolution set, depth set, channel set, and kernel size set, and acquire benchmarks for all child models in this limited space. This is followed by a fine-grained search phase, where we first pick the best network skeleton satisfying the given resource constraint found in the previous phase, and afterward randomly mutate its network-wise resolution, stage-wise depth, number of channels, and kernel sizes to further discover better network architectures. Finally, we directly utilize the weights from the single-stage model for the prompted child models with no retraining or finetuning.

## 4 Experiment

### 4.1 Experimental Settings

**Baseline Settings.** In our experiments, we use ResNet-18 as the default backbone. We perform 100-epoch pretraining before validation.

*Optimizer.* In our experiments, SGD is used for pretraining. A linear-scaling learning rate of $lr \times BatchSize \div 256$, with a base $lr = 0.03$, is used in our experiments. We adopt a cosine decay schedule to adjust the learning rate. The weight decay is set to be 0.0001 and the SGD momentum is 0.9.

*Projection MLP.* BN is applied to each fully connected (FC) layer of the projection MLP (in f) for our experiments. The output FC has no ReLU operation. The hidden FC of the projection is 2048-d. The Projection MLP holds 2 layers.

*Prediction MLP.* The prediction MLP (h) has BN applied to its hidden FC layers, but no BN or ReLUits is used in its output FC. The prediction MLP has 2 layers. The dimension of h's input and output (z and p) is $d_h = 2048$, and h's hidden layer's dimension is 512, which makes h a bottleneck structure.

**BigNAS Settings.** [13] In the training process of the supernet, we used SGD as an optimizer and a scheduler with cosine decay to adjust the learning rate. In the CIFAR10 dataset, our initial learning rate is set to 0.03, BatchSize is set to 512, and training time is set to 800 epochs. weight decay is set to 0.0005, and SGD mometunm is set to 0.9.

*Search Space.* We use the ResNet search space as the supernet. the min widths of supernet are set to be $[32, 32, 64, 128, 256]$, and the max widths of supernet are set to be $[64, 96, 160, 320, 640]$. The min depth of the supernet is set to be $[1, 1, 1, 1, 1]$, max depth of the supernet is set to be $[1, 2, 2, 3, 3]$. The min kernel size of the supernet is set to be $[3, 3, 3, 3, 3]$, the max kernel size of the supernet is set to be $[7, 3, 3, 3, 3]$.

**Validation Setting**

*DataSet.* We first performed baseline experiment on the CIFAR-10 dataset [11] to get the accuracy performance of a single contrastive learning model. We then applied the neural architecture search method to train a bunch of unsupervised submodels. For the CIFAR-10 dataset, we used 45000 elements for training, 5000 elements for validation, and 10,000 elements for testing.

*KNN Predictor.* We followe the setting in SimCLR [4], using the KNN predictor to get accuracy for our pretrained models. The temperature $knn_t$ is set to be 0.01 and cluster number $knn_k$ is set to be 200.

## 4.2   Experimental Results and Analysis

In this experiment, we conducted a search and evaluation of the network structure, shown in Fig. 4. In this experiment, we adopt our unsupervised NAS algorithm to search for a series of unsupervised architectures and use the greedy method to get the models under the Pareto boundary.

The results show that the network searched by using the multi-models target contrastive learning has better performance than Single training unsupervised models.

To further explore the performance of different networks under the same training set, we select three networks under different computation budgets and named these three networks UnBigNAS-Small, UnBigNAS-Medium, and UnBigNAS-Large respectively (as shown in Table 1).

Further experimental results show that UnBigNAS-Small, UnBigNAS-Medium, and UnBigNAS-Large exhibit better performance than the baseline

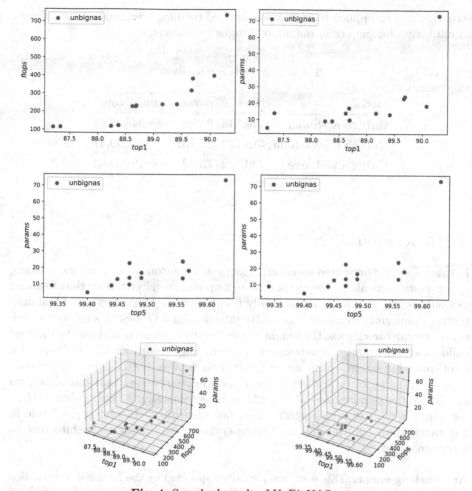

**Fig. 4.** Searched result of UnBigNAS

models, which also verifies our theory to some extent. There exist a search space that is capable of a contrastive learning method.

At the same time, by observing the experimental results in Table 1, it can be concluded that the amount of parameters also has a certain influence on the experimental results.

The experimental results show that in the multi-model mode, the model with relatively larger resource consumption UnBigNAS-Large shows better performance against confrontation. This also shows that, to a certain extent, there is a competitive relationship between the optimization of unsupervised accuracy and model parameters.

To some extent, our algorithm can boost the performance of a single architecture using a multi-model contrastive method. This also verifies that our algorithm can play a good role in automatic tuning in the design of unsupervised neural network architecture to a certain extent. At the same time, the searched structure can be applied to more unsupervised training scenarios under different computation budgets than manually designed methods.

**Table 1.** Models comparision

| Model | flops | params | top1 | top5 |
|---|---|---|---|---|
| UnBigNAS-Small | 120.545 | 9.025 | 88.24 | 99.34 |
| UnBigNAS-Medium | 318.124 | 22.852 | 89.67 | 99.47 |
| UnBigNAS-Large | 736.702 | 73.521 | 90.29 | 99.63 |

## 5  Conclusion

In this paper, we presented an effective method for autonomous machine learning of contrastive learning. The method is built upon a keen hypothesis that Encoder $f$ should belong to a functioning family $\mathbf{F}$ of functions $f$ within which $f$ can map pictures uniformly to higher spaces. By introducing a One-Shot supernet search space, we can directly use the weights from the single-stage model for the induced child models without any retraining or finetuning. Additionally, we designed a multi-model gradient optimization method to achieve better accuracy for contrastive training for multiple models. Experiments revealed that our algorithm can boost the performance of a single architecture using a contrastive method for multiple models, which verifies that our algorithm can play a good role in automatic tuning in the design of unsupervised neural network architecture to a certain extent.

**Acknowledgement.** This work was partially supported by the National Natural Science Foundation of China (61632011, 61876053, 62006062), the Shenzhen Foundational Research Funding (JCYJ20180507183527919), China Postdoctoral Science Foundation (2020M670912), Joint Lab of HITSZ and China Merchants Securities.

## References

1. Higgins, I., et al.: Beta-VAE: learning basic visual concepts with a constrained variational framework. In: ICLR 2017: International Conference on Learning Representations (2017)
2. Goodfellow, I., et al.: Generative adversarial nets. Adv. Neural Inf. Process. Syst. **27**(5), 2672–2680 (2014)
3. He, K., et al.: Momentum contrast for unsupervised visual representation learning. In: 2020 IEEE/CVF Conference on Computer Vision and Pattern Recognition (CVPR), pp. 9729–9738 (2020)
4. Chen, T., et al.: A simple framework for contrastive learning of visual representations. In: ICML 2020: 37th International Conference on Machine Learning, vol. 1, pp. 1597–1607 (2020)

5. Grill, J.-B., et al.: Bootstrap your own latent: a new approach to self-supervised learning. In: Advances in Neural Information Processing Systems, vol. 33, pp. 21271–21284 (2020)
6. Chen, X., He, K.: Exploring simple siamese representation learning. In: Proceedings of the IEEE/CVF Conference on Computer Vision and Pattern Recognition, pp. 15750–15758 (2020)
7. Zoph, B., et al.: Learning transferable architectures for scalable image recognition. In: Proceedings of the IEEE Conference on Computer Vision and Pattern Recognition, pp. 8697–8710 (2018)
8. Hu, J., Shen, L., Sun, G.: Squeeze-and-excitation networks. In: Proceedings of the IEEE Conference on Computer Vision and Pattern Recognition (CVPR), pp. 7132–7141 (2018)
9. Real, E., et al.: Regularized evolution for image classifier architecture search. In: Proceedings of the AAAI Conference on Artificial Intelligence, p. 4780–4789 (2019)
10. Liu, H., Simonyan, K., Yang, Y.: DARTS: differentiable architecture search. In: International Conference on Learning Representations (ICLR), p. 3 (2019)
11. Krizhevsky, A., Hinton, G.: Convolutional deep belief networks on CIFAR-10. Unpublished Manuscript **40**(7), 1–9 (2010)
12. Liu, C., et al.: Auto-DeepLab: hierarchical neural architecture search for semantic image segmentation. In: Proceedings of the IEEE Conference on Computer Vision and Pattern Recognition, p. 82–92 (2019)
13. Yu, J., et al.: BigNAS: scaling up neural architecture search with big single-stage models. In: Vedaldi, A., Bischof, H., Brox, T., Frahm, J.-M. (eds.) ECCV 2020. LNCS, vol. 12352, pp. 702–717. Springer, Cham (2020). https://doi.org/10.1007/978-3-030-58571-6_41

# Conversational Humor Identification Based on Adversarial Learning on Chinese Sitcoms

Wenbo Shang, Jing Wei, Runhui Song, Yan Xu, and Binyang Li[✉]

School of Cyber Science and Engineering, University of International Relations,
Beijing, China
byli@uir.edu.cn

**Abstract.** Humor computing aims to recognize, interpret, and generate humorous expressions based on computational models, which has become one of the key issues in the field of natural language processing. Humor computing is essential for artificial intelligence to make machines more humane. However, most research focuses on one-liner, and few research has paid attention to humor identification in conversations, that is conversational humor identification. Conversational humor identification faces the following challenges: 1. dataset is difficult to be constructed; 2. key features indicating conversational humorous expressions are hard to be captured by traditional ways. Our work is based on a Chinese sitcom dataset, which consists of all the dialogues of the sitcom. Punchlines referring to the part of dialogues play a role in making people laugh are also annotated in the dataset. Conversational humor identification is to identify the punchline. To do this, we propose a humor identification model based on Adversarial Learning, where the generator is able to produce sequences similar to punchlines, while the discriminator can learn the features to distinguish punchlines from non-humor dialogue. In this way, when given an input dialogue, the discriminator will classify whether it is a punchline for each sentence. We conduct experiments to assess the performance of our model, and we also compare the experimental results with some strong baselines. There are 25.4% improvement over BERT with respect of F1-score. Moreover, we also design ablation experiment to analyze different factors in conversational humor identification. And we discover that the generator plays a more important role in the model.

**Keywords:** Punchline identification · Adversarial learning · Reinforcement learning

## 1 Introduction

Humor is a special way of language expression, which plays an important role in resolving embarrassment, lightening the mood and promoting communication in daily life. Humor computing [19] is one of the emerging central issues in the field

© Springer Nature Switzerland AG 2022
R. Xu et al. (Eds.): ICCC 2021, LNCS 12992, pp. 24–34, 2022.
https://doi.org/10.1007/978-3-030-96419-1_3

of natural language processing in recent years, which mainly focuses on how to recognize, classify and generate humor.

In practical application scenarios, there are many forms of humor, including one-liner, conversational humor etc. However, most research [23,24] focuses on one-liner and few research [9,20] has paid attention to humor identification in conversations. Different from one-liner humor computing [23,24], conversational humor identification targets on identifying punchlines, which are the parts of dialogues playing a role in making people laugh. Conversational humor identification can be applied to a variety of scenarios, including chat robots, machine translation, children's educational software, and opinion mining, etc., which has far-reaching significance for the research in these related fields. Moreover, a humorous environment helps people cope with negative emotions such as stress, anxiety or depression, and enjoy the fun of interaction, thereby establishing more beneficial social relationships, which is conducive to the healthy development of society.

In this paper, we attempt to identify punchlines from conversations. It is very complex, and one of the key challenges is that existing methods are difficult to analyze the specific factors which make the expressions humorous. For example: *A: "Do you want to invite the two of us to go out and eat out? Come on, we are not outsiders!" B: "No, I'm just afraid to come back too late to eat our family meal."* In the above conversation, *A* thought that *B* was sending out an invitation to dinner, while *B* was just afraid that he would miss the dinner. There exists a punchline due to the semantic contrast between the two dialogues.

This phenomenon is called inconsistency, which refers to the discontinuity of contextual semantics [15]. Given a sentence, the following sentence does not meet people's expectations, which generates an unexpected and inverted effect. To judge if it is a punchline, a straightforward way is to measure the inconsistency. However, some inconsistent dialogues will be also caused by irrelevant contexts, such as *"I am eating an apple." "The stars in the sky are beautiful."*. It is difficult to directly measure the inconsistency for humor identification. So, we attempt to measure the degree of similarity between a sentence and a punchline. The more similar the generated sentence is to the punchline, the more possible it is to indicate humorous.

For this purpose, we propose a conversational humor identification model based on **Adversarial Learning** [12], using the metric of similarity to identify punchlines. In order for the model to heuristically learn the features of the punchline, we optimize the generator and the discriminator mutually. Generator can make generated sentences more and more similar to punchlines. While the process of generator and discriminator improving each other, the discriminator can learn the features to distinguish punchlines from non-humor dialogue. In this way, when given an input dialogue, the discriminator will classify whether it is a punchline for each sentence.

We conduct experiments based on a Chinese sitcom dataset, which consists of all the dialogues of the sitcom. We compare the experimental results against other baselines, and find that our method achieves the best performance, i.e., 47.9% with respect to F1-score. Moreover, we also conduct ablation experiments to analyze the influence of some factors, such as generator, fine-tuning. Compared with the pure discriminator (model without generator), there are 20.7% improvement by our model, indicating that the generator is a very important factor. Moreover, the discriminator really has indeed learned the features of the punchline in the process of mutual optimization with the generator, which leads to a more accurate identification. For the rigorousness of the experiment, we also have a trial to fine-tune the discriminator, and find that the experimental result is lower, indicating that there is a certain degree of textual similarity between punchline and non-punchline, which mislead the model.

## 2   Related Work

Early research in humor detection mainly used traditional machine learning methods (Naive Bayes, Perceptron, AdaBoost, etc.) combined with humor features (humor inconsistency, ambiguity, context, and other features) to solve the problem. Morales et al. [7] constructed multiple features based on a generative model, and used supervised learning to classify comments as humorous. The experimental results on the Yelp comment dataset show that the method of constructing features based on generative model is much more effective than previous method of feature construction.

However, traditional machine learning classifiers lack semantic understanding. In recent years, with the development of neural networks, more language models have been applied to humor computing Chen et al. [8] modified CNN by increasing the size and number of filters. They use the Highway Network architecture to implement a more accurate humor detection model. Many baselines have shown significant improvements in detecting different types of humorous situations.

Zhou et al. [9] proposed Pronunciation-attentive Contextualized Pun Recognition (PCPR) to construct a word representation that contains contextual information and speech information. In order to capture the phonetic structure of words, they decompose each word into a sequence of phonemes according to the pronunciation of the word, and homophones can have similar phoneme sets. However, their model only addresses the classification of English puns, not the classification of Chinese humorous texts. Fan et al. [10] proposed an end-to-end neural network called "Phonetics and Ambiguity Comprehension Gated Attention Network for Humor Recognition" to detect humor in text. This model captures voice information through CNN, combining bi-directional gated recursive unit (Bi-GRU) and attention mechanism to construct context and ambiguous word information. But this method is still unable to measure inconsistency, resulting in unsatisfactory model performance.

Inspired by SeqGAN [6], our proposed model is able to capture the features of humorous text heuristically, and then to optimize the discriminator separately, so that humor identification can be performed more effectively.

# 3   Methodology

## 3.1   Overview

Method shown in Fig. 2 is based on SeqGAN [6] model for conversational humor identification, aiming to classify humor and non-humor sentences based on a generative model. Our work trains adversarial network to endow generator with capability of generating punchlines and endow discriminator with capability of identifying whether a sequence is a punchline. The pipeline is shown in Fig. 1.

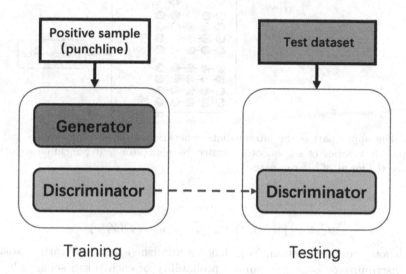

**Fig. 1.** Pipeline: on the left is the training module, and on the right is the testing module with the discriminator alone.

## 3.2   Training Based on SeqGAN

Assuming that the result generated by a $\theta$-parameterized generator is a series of sequence $Y = \{y_1, ......, y_T\}$, $y_i$ represents a token in the Y sequence. The real-world data is a series of punchline sequences $X = \{x_1, ......, x_N\}$, $x_i$ represents a token in the X sequence. The problem is denoted as follows:

The generator parameters are randomly initialized. The process of generating is based on reinforcement learning [14]. Assuming that in timestep $t$, the current state S, which refers to current generated tokens, can be represented by $S = \{s_1, s_2, ..., s_{t-1}\}$ , namely $S_{1:t-1}$. At this timestep $t$, next action is to select next token from candidate set $R = \{r_1, r_2, ......, r_t\}$, containing several candidate tokens. Then, if $r_i$ is selected as the next token, it will be represented as $s_t$. For the reward of each action, discriminator will estimate probability of whether a complete sequence generated by Monte Carlo search [13] involving this action will be judged as a punchline, in the current state S, if next token is $r_i$.

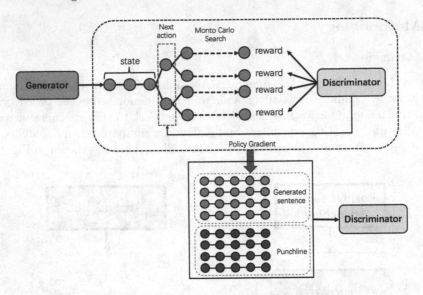

**Fig. 2.** The upper part is the intermediate generation process of generator, and the lower part is a series of sequences generated by generator and punchline sequences jointly as the input of discriminator.

$$Q(S = \{s_1, s_2, ..., s_{t-1}\}, a = s_t) = D(Y_{1:T}) \tag{1}$$

**a** denotes the next action, $Y_{1:T}$ denotes a finished sequence with T tokens. Since discriminator cannot eliminate probability of each token separately, the input is necessarily a complete sequence. Therefore, Monte Carlo search [13] is used to iterate each candidate token $r_i$ N times to generate several complete sequences as input of discriminator.

$$\{Y_{1:T}^1, Y_{1:T}^2, ..., Y_{1:T}^N\} = MC(Y_{1:t}^{r_i}; N) \tag{2}$$

$Y_{1:t}^{r_i}$ denotes an unfinished sequence with t tokens for each candidate token $r_i$. N denotes number of iterations.

Each candidate token will correspond to N generated sequences. Input these N sequences into discriminator, and then discriminator will estimate the probability of each sequence, that is, reward. For the next step, calculate the average value of N rewards as the final reward of each candidate token if it is the next action.

If the candidate token is the last word that needs to be generated in a complete sequence, the reward is equal to the discriminator's estimated probability of the complete sequence containing the candidate word [13].

$$Q(S_{1:t-1}, a = r_i) = \frac{\sum_{n=1}^{N} D(Y_{1:T}^n)}{N} \tag{3}$$

After that, the results of reward value are passed to the generator via policy gradient update. Then, generator iterates continuously to generate next token until a complete sentence is generated. When generator completes generating, input punchline sequences X and generated sequences Y to discriminator [12] to train.

The objective function of the discriminator is as follows.

$$\min -E_{Y \sim p_{data}}\left[\log D(Y)\right] - E_{Y \sim G_\theta}\left[\log(1 - D(Y))\right] \tag{4}$$

$P_{data}$ represents punchline data. $G_\theta$ represents the policy of generator, which we will introduce below. Each time when a new discriminator has completed iteration, update the parameters of generator by policy gradient.

## 3.3   Policy Gradient

When generator generates next token, the goal is to maximize the expected reward calculated according to each candidate token in the current state $s_t$. The goal of generator model (policy) [11] $G_\theta(r_i|S_{1:t-1})$ is to generate a sequence from starting state $s_\theta$, maximizing its expected final reward.

$$J(\theta) = E(R_T|s_{t-1}, \theta) = \sum_{r_i \in R} G_\theta(r_i|S_{1:t-1}\}) \cdot Q(S_{1:t-1}\}, r_i) \tag{5}$$

J($\theta$) represents the objective function of generator, $R_T$ represents the reward of a sequence that has been generated, $\theta$ represents the parameters of generator, $G_\theta$ represents the generator's generation policy, and Q(s,a) is the action-value function of a sequence, the expected accumulative reward starting from state s , selecting action a, and then following the policy of $G_\theta$. Therefore, the gradient of generator objective function [11] can be denoted as:

$$\nabla_\theta J(\theta) = \sum_{t=1}^{T} E_{S_{1:t-1} \sim G_\theta}\left[\sum_{r_i \in R} \nabla_\theta G_\theta(r_i|S_{1:t-1}) \cdot Q(S_{1:t-1}, r_i)\right] \tag{6}$$

After calculating the gradient value, update the parameters of the generator. The formula is as follows:

$$\theta \longleftarrow \theta + \alpha \nabla_\theta J(\theta) \tag{7}$$

$\alpha_h$ is the learning rate at h-th step, $\theta$ denotes parameters of generator, of course, some optimized gradient algorithms can also be used, such as Adam.

## 4   Experiments

### 4.1   Dataset and Metrics

To evaluate the performance of our proposed method, extensive experiments were conducted based on a publicly available dataset which is collected from a famous

Chinese situational comedy *I Love My Family*. Depending on the scene and the plot changing by the timeline, the sitcom is divided into several dialogues. A dialogue consists of different utterances which from different characters and every utterance has a label humorous or non-humorous. Table 1 shows the statistics of dataset.

**Table 1.** Dataset introduction

| Dataset | Train | Dev | Test | Total |
|---|---|---|---|---|
| Dialogues | 348 | 43 | 128 | 519 |
| Utterances | 12,677 | 1,632 | 4794 | 19,103 |
| Dialogues' Avg.len | 36.34 | 37.95 | 37.45 | 36.81 |
| Utterances' Avg.len | 9.99 | 10.49 | 10.02 | 10.04 |
| Percentage of humorous (%) | 28.76 | 26.23 | 28.04 | 28.36 |

**Metrics:** Given a dialogue, the aim of the task is to learn a binary classification to detect whether an utterance is humorous or not. To fully evaluate the performance of our model on this task, two types of metrics are used at different levels. In utterance level, F1score is suitable and the calculation formula is as follows:

$$F_1 = \frac{2 \times P \times R}{P + R} \tag{8}$$

Where P and R represent precision and recall respectively. In this classification task, the precision for a class is the number of true positives divided by the total number of elements labelled as belonging to the positive class. Recall in this context is defined as the number of true positives divided by the total number of elements that actually belong to the positive class.

## 4.2   Comparison Methods

We compare our proposed model with the following approaches:

**LSTM:** [22] Long Short-Term Memory is a type of RNN (Recurrent Neural Network). [1] A common LSTM unit is composed of a cell, an input gate, an output gate and a forget gate. LSTM is well suited for modeling temporal data, such as conversation data, due to its network architecture

**Bi-LSTM:** BiLSTM [2] stands for Bi-directional Short-Term Memory, which is a combination of forward LSTM and backward LSTM. In this task, a single layer BiLSTM is used to model each utterance as a sequence of words and predict each utterance's label with a softmax function.

**BC-LSTM:** BC-LSTM means background LSTM network, which constructs a single utterance with its paragraph context.

**BERT:** [5] The full name of BERT is Bidirectional Encoder Representation from Transformers, which is a pre-trained language representation model. BERT uses masked language model (MLM) for pre-training and bi-directional Transformer components to build the entire model, thus it can generate a deep bi-directional language representation that incorporates left and right contextual information. In this method, the humor identification task is treated as a classification task of the pre-trained model to fine-tune the BERT [4].

**SVM:** [21] Support-vector Machines are supervised learning models with associated learning algorithms that analyze data for classification and regression analysis. In this method, SVM is used to deal with the binary classification problem of whether it is a punchline.

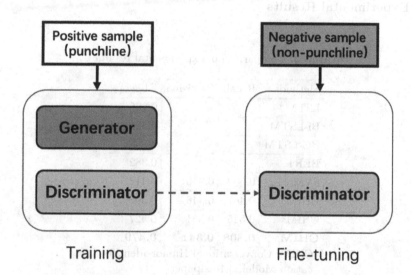

**Fig. 3.** Fine-tuning: the part on the left is our work, and the right one is fine-tuning. Trained discriminator's parameters are shared with the fine-tuned discriminator.

### 4.3 Ablation Experiment

We guess that there is a bias in the model training process. There is a deviation between actual ability of the discriminator and expected ability. In fact, generator in the model has weak capabilities and cannot generate sentences that are similar to punchlines. Because an important feature of humor is inconsistency, which means, if there is inconsistent semantics in a sentence then it can trigger humor. An important measure of text generation is fluency, which evaluates the logic and readability of generated sentences. Therefore, if generator has the ability to generate a humorous sentence as we expected, then generator needs to balance the relationship between inconsistency and fluency for realizing semantic inconsistency under the premise of fluent language and coherence semantic. But in fact, it is difficult for a generator to achieve such an ideal state. As a result, generator cannot generate a punchline, or even a fluent sentence over punchline dataset, which may lead to a bias in the discriminator, that is, while identifying the punchline, it largely recognizes whether a sentence is generated by a machine.

Therefore, in order to prove our conjecture, we fine-tune the discriminator (shown in Fig. 3). We input the negative sample, i.e., non-punchline, into the discriminator for training, to correct the bias of the discriminator, and give discriminator ability to discriminate whether a sentence is a punchline.

### 4.4  Experimental Results

Table 2. Comparison of experimental results

| Methods | Recall | Precision | F1-score |
|---------|--------|-----------|----------|
| LSTM | – | – | 0.286 |
| Bi-LSTM | – | – | 0.326 |
| BC-LSTM | – | – | 0.358 |
| BERT | – | – | 0.382 |
| SVM | 0.500 | 0.350 | 0.412 |
| CHIM* | 0.467 | 0.346 | 0.397 |
| CHIM$^\sharp$ | 0.545 | 0.351 | 0.427 |
| **CHIM** | **0.808** | **0.341** | **0.479** |

[a] CHIM: Conversational Humor Identification Model in this paper
[b] CHIM*: without generator
[c] CHIM$^\sharp$: with fine-tuning

The overall results were shown in Table 2. It was obviously that our proposed model significantly outperformed the other models in two evaluation metrics. The BC-LSTM network that models the context of the paragraph shows a boost compared to the single-layer bi-directional LSTM network that only targets one sentence of dialogue, suggesting that the information learned from the context helps with humor recognition in the paragraph. However due to network structure, the information in long texts is gradually forgotten in LSTM network even though bidirectional networks improve this situation. The fine-tuned

BERT model shows strong performance with the attention mechanism in this task. To our surprise, the experimental results of SVM on this task are better than those of BERT. Both the serialization model and the attention mechanism model treat this task as a text classification problem, the proposed model in this paper provide a generator to parody writing humorous utterances. The utterances generated by the model contain the features that the machine has learned about humor. Then the discriminator is responsible for distinguishing humorous utterance, to some extent these machine-generated sentences play a data-enhancing role in the discriminatory process.

To investigate whether our generator produces high-quality sentences that have a positive effect on the discriminator, we also perform a rigorous ablation experiment. Table 3 shows the results of the ablation experiment. Without generator, the F1-score of the discriminator is significantly reduced which signify the importance of generator in whole model. Compare the discriminator without fine-tuning step, the F1-score is higher. The oblation results show that the special fine-tuning we designed for our model can mislead the discriminator.

# 5  Conclusion

In this paper, we proposed a humor detection method based on SeqGAN. This method can heuristically learn features of humorous text. As far as we know, this is the first work based on SeqGAN model to implement a humor identification task. In our data experiments, we used comprehensive evaluation metrics to explicitly illustrate the superiority of our method over strong baselines. At the same time, we also did ablation experiments to analyze the impact of different variables on the model identification effect. In our future work, we hope that we can combine contextual role information to enhance the model's understanding of the text, so as to achieve better experimental results.

**Acknowledgements.** We would like to thank for Xurui Sun, Yuan Chang, Chongyan Zhou, Aocheng Zhang, Yaoyao Qin, Tianyun Zhong, Xueyao Zhang, Ruiqi Cao, Jundan Zhou, Shuoyu Shi, Jiayue Bao, Bingqian Wen, Jinhui Zhao, Yize Zhao, Xinlu Li, Linjie Shi annotating the dataset. This work was partially supported by the National Natural Science Foundation of China (Grant number: 61976066), Beijing Natural Science Foundation (Grant number: 4212031), and the Fundamental Research Fund for the Central Universities (Grant numbers: 2019GA35, 2019GA43, 3262021T23).

# References

1. Schuster, M., Paliwal, K.K.: Bidirectional recurrent neural networks. IEEE Trans. Signal Process. **45**(11), 2673–2681 (1997)
2. Shi, X., et al.: Convolutional LSTM Network: A Machine Learning Approach for Precipitation Nowcasting. MIT Press, Cambridge (2015)
3. Devlin, J., et al.: BERT: Pre-training of Deep Bidirectional Transformers for Language Understanding. CoRR. abs/1810.04805 (2018)
4. Vaswani, A., et al.: Attention Is All You Need. arXiv (2017)

5. Sun, C., Qiu, X., Xu, Y., Huang, X.: How to fine-tune BERT for text classification? In: Sun, M., Huang, X., Ji, H., Liu, Z., Liu, Y. (eds.) CCL 2019. LNCS (LNAI), vol. 11856, pp. 194–206. Springer, Cham (2019). https://doi.org/10.1007/978-3-030-32381-3_16

6. Yu, L., et al.: SeqGAN: sequence generative adversarial nets with policy gradient. In: AAAI Conference on Artificial Intelligence, pp. 2852–2858 (2017)

7. Morales, A., Zhai, C.: Identifying humor in reviews using background text sources. In: Proceedings of the 2017 Conference on Empirical Methods in Natural Language Processing, pp. 492–501 (2017)

8. Chen, P.Y., Soo, V.W.: Humor recognition using deep learning. In: Proceedings of the 2018 Conference of the North American Chapter of the Association for Computational Linguistics: Human Language Technologies, vol. 2 (Short Papers), pp. 113–117 (2018)

9. Zhou, Y., Jiang, J.Y., Zhao, J., Chang, K.W., Wang, W.: The Boating Store Had Its Best Sail Ever: Pronunciation-attentive Contextualized Pun Recognition. arXiv preprint arXiv:2004.14457 (2020)

10. Diao, Y., Fan, X., Yang, L., et al.: Phonetics and ambiguity comprehension gated attention network for humor recognition. Complexity **2020**, 1–9 (2020)

11. Sutton, R.S., et al.: Policy gradient methods for reinforcement learning with function approximation. In: NIPS, pp. 1057–1063 (1999)

12. Goodfellow, I., et al.: Generative adversarial nets. In: NIPS, pp. 2672–2680 (2014)

13. Silver, D., Huang, A., Maddison, C.J., Guez, A., Sifre, L., et al.: Mastering the game of go with deep neural networks and tree search. Nature **529**(7587), 484–489 (2016)

14. Williams, R.J.: Simple statistical gradient-following algorithms for connectionist reinforcement learning. Mach. Learn. **8**(3–4), 229–256 (1992)

15. Reyes, A., Rosso, P., Buscaldi, D.: From humor recognition to irony detection: the figurative language of social media. Data Knowl. Eng. **74**, 1–12 (2012)

16. Mihalcea, R., Pulman, S.: Characterizing humour: an exploration of features in humorous texts. In: Gelbukh, A. (ed.) CICLing 2007. LNCS, vol. 4394, pp. 337–347. Springer, Heidelberg (2007). https://doi.org/10.1007/978-3-540-70939-8_30

17. Yang, D., Lavie, A., Dyer, C., Hovy, E.: Humor recognition and humor anchor extraction. In: Proceedings of the 2015 Conference on Empirical Methods in Natural Language Processing, EMNLP 2015. The Association for Computational Linguistics, pp. 2367–2376 (2015)

18. Attardo, S.: Linguistic theories of humor. Language **72**(72), 45–64 (1996)

19. Purandare, A., Litman, D.: Humor: prosody analysis and automatic recognition for F*R*I*E*N*D*S*. In: Proceedings of the Conference on Empirical Methods in Natural Language Processing, pp. 208–215. ACM, New York (2006)

20. Fan, X., et al.: Humor detection via an internal and external neural network. Neurocomputing **394**, 105–111 (2020)

21. Cortes, C., Vapnik, V.: Support-vector networks. Mach. Learn. **20**, 273–297 (1995)

22. Hochreiter, S., Schmidhuber, J.: Long short-term memory. Neural Comput. **9**, 1735–1780 (1997)

23. Oliva, J., Serrano, J.I., Del Castillo, M.D., Iglesias Á.: SyMSS: a syntax-based measure for short-text semantic similarity. DKE 390–405 (2011)

24. Yang, D., et al.: Humor recognition and humor anchor extraction. In: EMNLP, pp. 2367–2376. Lisbon (2015)

# A Novel Linguistic-Aware Memory Structure for Enhancing the Response Generation

Pengda Si[1($\boxtimes$)], Yiru Wang[2($\boxtimes$)], and Yujiu Yang[1($\boxtimes$)]

[1] Shenzhen International Graduate School, Tsinghua University, Shenzhen, China
spd18@mails.tsinghua.edu.cn , yang.yujiu@sz.tsinghua.edu.cn
[2] Tencent Inc., Shenzhen, China

**Abstract.** People will think of conversation experiences during a chat. Inspired by the phenomena, some previous works exploit relevant conversation utterances to enhance the response generation process. However, these methods only focus on semantic information while ignoring linguistic information. As a result, relevant sentences are not fully utilized. To address the problem, we design a novel memory structure to store linguistic information. Specifically, we conduct a memory bank on the relevant utterances, consisting a series of key-value pairs. And the memory structure is combined during the generation process. We conduct experiments on two public conversation datasets, and the results demonstrate the effectiveness of our memory structure.

## 1 Introduction

Although the generative dialogue model has been improved and achieved pretty good performance these years, there still exit many problems, which will bore and interrupt the conversation [1, 2]. Inspired by the fact that humans give responses based on their dialogue experiences, some previous works suggest introducing relevant conversation utterances [3, 4] to enhance the generation process. They usually construct memory structures to store and exploit information of relevant utterances. However, these memory structures only focus on semantic information while ignoring linguistic information. We argue this method is not enough to use relevant sentences fully and can be further improved.

A sentence contains both semantic and linguistic information. Its semantic information refers to the meaning of the entire sentence, while its linguistic information refers to the order of words. An example is presented in Fig. 1. For the sentence "I like eating apple", its linguistic information means how to give the next word according to the existing sequence, such as from "I like" to infer "eating". Obviously, the linguistic information is more consistent with the autoregressive form of response the generation process.

In order to introduce linguistic information, we design a novel memory structure. Specifically, we first search for several relevant utterances for the given post.

© Springer Nature Switzerland AG 2022
R. Xu et al. (Eds.): ICCC 2021, LNCS 12992, pp. 35–43, 2022.
https://doi.org/10.1007/978-3-030-96419-1_4

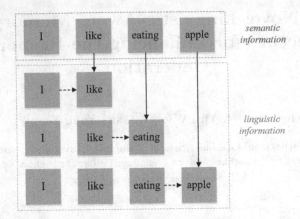

**Fig. 1.** The example contains both semantic information and linguistic information.

Then, based on these relevant utterances, we construct a memory bank that consists of a series of key-value pairs. The value and key correspond to the word and the previous text sequence, respectively. Finally, the memory structure is introduced to the response generation process. Besides, a gate structure is applied to control the participation of memory information.

We conduct our experiments on two popular dialog datasets: Dailydialog [5] and Opensubtitles [6]. Both automatic and human evaluations demonstrate our proposed method outperforms several baselines, indicating the effectiveness of our memory structure.

We can summarize our contributions into two folds:

– We present a novel memory structure to introduce linguistic information.
– Experimental results on two datasets show the effectiveness of our method.

## 2    Related Work

The open-domain response generation task has attracted much attention since the sequence to sequence (seq2seq) architecture was proposed [7]. As large pre-trained models, such as BERT [8], GPT-2 [9] appear, open-domain chatbot performs better and better. However, there still exist a series of challenges [1,2] and a solution is to exploit relevant utterances. Wang [10,11] introduces topic to help generation. Pandey [3] proposes to introduce relevant conversation utterances into the generation process. Pei and Li [4] develops the idea and proposes a model that utilizes information of relevant utterances at each step of the generation process. Wu [12], Yang [13] combine the retrieval method and the generation method, and their methods generate responses based on the relevant candidates. However, these works only utilize semantic information and ignore linguistic information. We further improve this method and introduce linguistic information into generation.

# 3　Method

## 3.1　Overview

In general, the dialog generation task can be defined as follows: **Given the post** $x$**, we aim to generate its response** $y$. In other words, our task is generating the best hypothesis $y'$ which maximizes the following conditional probability:

$$y' = argmax P(y|x) \tag{1}$$

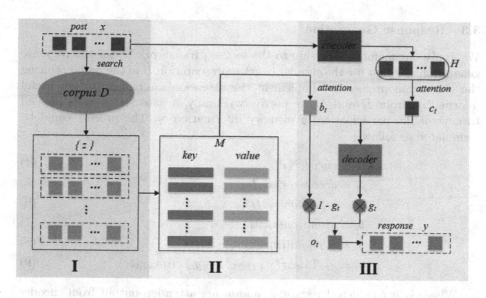

**Fig. 2.** The pipeline of our method.

　　Our pipeline is presented in Fig. 2, which could be split into three steps. Firstly, we search for several relevant utterances $\{z\}$ in dialog corpus $D$ according to the post $x$. Then, we construct a memory structure $M$ on $z$, which consists of a series of key-value pairs. Finally, we utilize information from $M$ to generate the response $y$. In the rest of this section, we describe the memory structure $M$ and how we exploit it in detail.

## 3.2　Memory Structure

Given the post $x$, we firstly search for several relevant utterances $\{z\}$, then construct a memory bank $M$ based on $\{z\}$. For a sentence $u$, its linguistic information refers to how to give the next work according to the previous text sequence. Thus, we construct a series of key-value pairs to store linguistic information of relevant utterances. Keys store the feature of the previous sequence while values store the feature of the current word. Specifically, we employ two architectures as two functions $f_{key}$ and $f_{value}$ to encode them, respectively. For the $j$-th key-value pair, we get key $k_j$ and value $v_j$ as follows:

$$k_j = f_{key}(w_1, w_2, \cdots, w_{j-1}) \tag{2}$$
$$v_j = f_{value}(w_j) \tag{3}$$

Where $w_j$ refers to $j$-th word in $u$. For a sentence $u$ with length $|u|$, we could construct $|u|$ key-value pairs. Therefore, for relevant utterances $\{z\}$, the size of our memory structure is $\sum_{u \in \{z\}} |u|$. We use $|M|$ to represent it for simplicity.

### 3.3 Response Generation

We apply our memory structure to the seq2seq framework [7] for the response generation. We first use the encoder to get representation $H$ of the post $x$. During the generation process, we implement the attention mechanism to get useful information from $H$ and $M$, respectively. Finally, a gate vector $g_t$ is applied to control the participation of memory information $b_t$. The process could be formulated as follows:

$$H = encoder(x) \tag{4}$$
$$s_{t+1} = decoder(s_t, c_t, b_t) \tag{5}$$
$$c_t = attention(s_t, H) \tag{6}$$
$$b_t = attention(s_t, M) \tag{7}$$
$$g_t = sigmoid(linear([s_{t+1}, b_t])) \tag{8}$$
$$o_t = g_t \cdot linear(s_{t+1}) + (1 - g_t) \cdot linear(b_t) \tag{9}$$

Where $s_t$ is $t$-th decoder state, $c_t$ and $b_t$ are attention output from encoder state $H$ and memory structure $M$, respectively. $linear$ is one-layer linear network and $g_t$ is the gate vector between $[0, 1]$. $o_t$ is the output of decoder.

## 4    Experiment

### 4.1    Datasets

We conduct experiments on two popular corpora, DailyDialog [5] and Opensubtitles [6]. DailyDialog is a high-quality conversation dataset in which the data is crawled from websites for English learners, and OpenSubtitles is a giant collection of movie subtitles. We split both datasets into single turn context-response pairs. We control the sentence length between 3 and 30. The information of datasets we use for our experiments is given in Table 1.

**Table 1.** Statistics information of two corpus in our experiments

| Corpus | Train | Valid | Test | Vocab size |
|--------|-------|-------|------|------------|
| DailyDialog | 70170 | 6690 | 6300 | 15000 |
| Opensubtitles | 404458 | 16750 | 16793 | 30000 |

## 4.2 Baselines

We choose three classical models similar to our model as baselines.

- **S2SA:** It apply the attention mechanism to the Seq2Seq model [14].
- **EED:** It uses an additional encoder to represent relevant sentences, then combine the representation with the original post text representation as the start state for generation process [3].
- **S2SPMN:** It utilizes semantic information of relevant sentences to help generation at each decode step [4].

For fairness, we don't compare our model with large pretrained models, such as BERT [8] and GPT-2 [9].

And we adopt several standard metrics to compare the responses generated by different models. Specifically, we adopt **Dist** [1] to evaluate the diversity of responses. **Bleu** [15] and **Embedding Metrics** [16] are used to measure the relevance between the generated responses and the ground truth.

## 4.3 Implement Details

We use the pretrained embedding vectors from Google News to initialize the embedding vector [17], which size is 300. Hidden size, batch size, and dropout are set to 512, 32, and 0.2, respectively. We use the TF-IDF feature to search for relevant utterances in the dialogue corpus, and the number is set to 3. The loss function is a general cross-entropy function, and we choose Adam as an optimizer with a 0.001 learning rate and 0.96 decay rate. Meanwhile, the gradient does not exceed 5 during training.

We utilize one-layer LSTM [18] to implement encoder and decoder in our response generation model. We adopt another LSTM network to implement function $f_{key}$. For the function $f_{value}$, we use a linear layer.

# 5 Evaluation

## 5.1 Evaluation by Different Metrics

Table 2 displays the evaluation results. Our model achieves the highest diversity scores on both corpora, which means that our model could give more informative responses. Our model also gets the highest BLeU score and embedding score on the DailyDialog corpus, indicating that our model's responses are more relevant to the ground truth. On the Opensubtitles corpus, although our model does not achieve the highest score in several metrics, it is still competitive.

**Table 2.** Automatic evaluation results of generated responses

| Model | BLEU | | Embedding metric | | | Dist | |
|---|---|---|---|---|---|---|---|
| | BLEU-3 | BLEU-4 | Ave. | Gre. | Ext. | Dist-3 | Dist-s |
| **DailyDialog** | | | | | | | |
| S2SA | 0.0105 | 0.0058 | 0.574 | 2.530 | 0.379 | 4266 | 2592 |
| S2SPMN | 0.0110 | 0.0061 | 0.576 | 2.504 | 0.382 | 4081 | 3025 |
| EED | 0.0104 | 0.0055 | 0.571 | 2.528 | 0.378 | 2833 | 1971 |
| Ours | **0.0136** | **0.0075** | **0.581** | **2.532** | **0.383** | **5310** | **3227** |
| **Opensubtitles** | | | | | | | |
| S2SA | 0.0163 | 0.0091 | 0.497 | 2.085 | 0.348 | 1317 | 1620 |
| S2SPMN | 0.0180 | 0.0099 | **0.509** | 2.105 | **0.354** | 1436 | 1695 |
| EED | 0.0173 | 0.0096 | 0.506 | **2.118** | **0.354** | 1563 | 1628 |
| Ours | **0.0186** | **0.0107** | 0.493 | 2.104 | 0.347 | **1923** | **2626** |

## 5.2 Human Evaluation

Since automatic metrics for open-domain responses may not be consistent with human perceptions, we further recruit six annotators for human evaluation. We randomly select 100 responses generated by different models on the Dailydialog test set. Responses generated by different models are randomly shuffled for each annotator. For each case, annotators are asked to make judgments from three aspects: **Fluency, Relevance and Informativeness**.

Manual evaluation results are presented in Table 3. We can see that all models get high fluent scores in the fluency aspect. Among them, S2SA gives the highest fluency score. The proposed model gets far higher scores for relevance and information richness than the other three baselines, which indicates that our model could generate more on-topic and informative responses.

**Table 3.** Human evaluation scores of generated resposnes

| Model | Fluency | Relevance | Informativeness |
|---|---|---|---|
| S2SA | **92.00** | 63.83 | 43.17 |
| S2SPMN | 88.67 | 58.17 | 40.00 |
| EED | 91.83 | 59.33 | 44.00 |
| Ours | 91.17 | **65.33** | **48.17** |

From evaluation results by automatic metrics and human annotators, we now confirm that our model with the designed memory structure outperforms three baselines and could generate better responses. Considering that S2SPMN and EED models utilize semantic information while our model utilizes linguistic information, we could infer that linguistic information is more helpful for the response generation process.

## 5.3   Case Study

Table 4 presents two examples. In the first case, the post describes something challenging. Our proposed model generates a relevant response to the post and gives the word "difficult" that matches "tough" in the post. However, the other three baselines give general responses. The second post is asking something about the weather report. We can see that only our model could understand the keyword "weather report" in the post and give a corresponding response, "5 degrees centigrade". And the other three baselines give weird responses.

**Table 4.** Two Cases of responses generated by different models

| #1 post | Wow That's interesting. It must be **tough** |
|---|---|
| **Human** | It's a bit difficult to find vegetarian friendly restaurants sometimes, but since more and more people are or nowadays, it's getting a bit less difficult |
| **S2SA** | Yes I think so |
| **S2SPMN** | Yeah I think so |
| **EED** | Yeah I guess |
| **Ours** | Yeah. It is **very difficult** to learn about it. |
| **#2 post** | Well, what's the **weather report**? |
| **Human** | Sunny and mild today, cloudy and rainy tomorrow |
| **S2SA** | It's a feature film |
| **S2SPMN** | It's the most important day |
| **EED** | It's about fifteen minutes'walk |
| **Ours** | It's about **5 degrees centigrade** |

The above two cases indicate that our models can give more on-topic and informative responses. The results are consistent with automatic metric evaluation and human evaluation, showing our proposed memory structure helps to give higher quality responses. We could also infer from the cases that linguistic information plays a vital role in response generation.

## 6   Conclusion

In this paper, we design a memory structure to enhance open-domain response generation. The structure stores linguistic information of relevant utterances. Experiments on large-scale corpora show that the proposed models generate responses with higher quality, proving the effectiveness of our method.

# References

1. Li, J., Galley, M., Brockett, C., Gao, J., Dolan, B.: A diversity-promoting objective function for neural conversation models. In: NAACL HLT 2016, The 2016 Conference of the North American Chapter of the Association for Computational Linguistics: Human Language Technologies, The Association for Computational Linguistics, pp. 110–119 (2016)
2. Huang, M., Zhu, X., Gao, J.: Challenges in building intelligent open-domain dialog systems. ACM Trans. Inf. Syst. **38**(3), 21:1–21:32 (2020)
3. Pandey, G., Contractor, D., Kumar, V., Joshi, S.: Exemplar encoder-decoder for neural conversation generation. In: Proceedings of the 56th Annual Meeting of the Association for Computational Linguistics, ACL 2018, Association for Computational Linguistics, pp. 1329–1338 (2018)
4. Pei, J., Li, C.: S2SPMN: a simple and effective framework for response generation with relevant information. In: Proceedings of the 2018 Conference on Empirical Methods in Natural Language Processing, EMNLP 2018, Association for Computational Linguistics, pp. 745–750 (2018)
5. Li, Y., Su, H., Shen, X., Li, W., Cao, Z., Niu, S.: Dailydialog: a manually labelled multi-turn dialogue dataset. In: Proceedings of the Eighth International Joint Conference on Natural Language Processing, IJCNLP 2017 - Volume 1: Long Papers, Asian Federation of Natural Language Processing, pp. 986–995 (2017)
6. Tiedemann, J.: Parallel data, tools and interfaces in OPUS. In: Proceedings of the Eighth International Conference on Language Resources and Evaluation, LREC 2012, European Language Resources Association (ELRA), pp. 2214–2218 (2012)
7. Sutskever, I., Vinyals, O., Le, Q.V.: Sequence to sequence learning with neural networks. In: Annual Conference on Neural Information Processing Systems 2014, NeurIPS 2014, pp. 3104–3112 (2014)
8. Devlin, J., Chang, M., Lee, K., Toutanova, K.: BERT: pre-training of deep bidirectional transformers for language understanding. In: Proceedings of the 2019 Conference of the North American Chapter of the Association for Computational Linguistics: Human Language Technologies, Association for Computational Linguistics, pp. 4171–4186 (2019)
9. Radford, A., Wu, J., Child, R., Luan, D., Amodei, D., Sutskever, I.: Language models are unsupervised multitask learners. OpenAI blog **1**(8), 9 (2019)
10. Wang, Y., Si, P., Lei, Z., Yang, Y.: Topic enhanced controllable CVAE for dialogue generation (student abstract). In: The Thirty-Fourth AAAI Conference on Artificial Intelligence, AAAI 2020, The Thirty-Second Innovative Applications of Artificial Intelligence Conference, IAAI 2020, The Tenth AAAI Symposium on Educational Advances in Artificial Intelligence, pp. 13955–13956, EAAI 2020, New York, NY, USA, 7–12 February 2020, AAAI Press (2020)
11. Wang, Y., Si, P., Lei, Z., Xun, G., Yang, Y.: HSCJN: a holistic semantic constraint joint network for diverse response generation. Comput. Speech Lang. **65**, 101135 (2021)
12. Wu, Y., Wei, F., Huang, S., Wang, Y., Li, Z., Zhou, M.: Response generation by context-aware prototype editing. In: The Thirty-Third AAAI Conference on Artificial Intelligence, pp. 7281–7288, AAAI2019, AAAI Press (2019)
13. Yang, L., et al.: A hybrid retrieval-generation neural conversation model. In: Proceedings of the 28th ACM International Conference on Information and Knowledge Management, pp. 1341–1350, CIKM 2019, ACM (2019)

14. Bahdanau, D., Cho, K., Bengio, Y.: Neural machine translation by jointly learning to align and translate. In: 3rd International Conference on Learning Representations, ICLR 2015 (2015)
15. Chen, B., Cherry, C.: A systematic comparison of smoothing techniques for sentence-level BLEU. In: Proceedings of the Ninth Workshop on Statistical Machine Translation, WMT@ACL 2014, The Association for Computer Linguistics, pp. 362–367 (2014)
16. Liu, C., Lowe, R., Serban, I., Noseworthy, M., Charlin, L., Pineau, J.: How NOT to evaluate your dialogue system: an empirical study of unsupervised evaluation metrics for dialogue response generation. In: Proceedings of the 2016 Conference on Empirical Methods in Natural Language Processing, EMNLP 2016, The Association for Computational Linguistics, pp. 2122–2132 (2016)
17. Pennington, J., Socher, R., Manning, C.D.: Glove: global vectors for word representation. In: Moschitti, A., Pang, B., Daelemans, W. (eds.) Proceedings of the 2014 Conference on Empirical Methods in Natural Language Processing, pp. 1532–1543. EMNLP 2014, ACL (2014)
18. Ciaccia, P., Maio, D., Vacca, G.P.: An analytical short- and long-term memory model of presynaptic plasticity. Biol. Cybern. 67(4), 335–345 (1992)

# Robotic Arm Movement Compliance Detection

Hengyi Zhou, Cheng Cai[✉], and Xuhui Li

School of Electronic Information Engineering, Shanghai Dianji University, Shanghai, China
caic@sdju.edu.cn

**Abstract.** In the Digital Twin design of CloudMinds Robot, there is no collision detection. When migrating human motion to CloudMinds Robot's motion, if collision detection is not performed, check whether the migrated motion is compliant, which will cause damage to CloudMinds Robot. This solution will be designed and modeled on the Webots open source platform, reproduce the CloudMinds Robot in the same scale, and control the loading action of the robotic arm to solve the collision problem. It will also timely feedback the collision information and the motor on the robotic arm under the premise of not passing through the model. The angle of rotation will also have a warning light to remind the collision. This research plan provides a solution for migrating human actions to robots in the digital twin design of CloudMinds Robots, and also provides a solution for industrial robots that can be simulated and tested in the digital twin environment of Webots.

**Keywords:** Webots · Robotic arm · Positive kinematics

## 1 Introduction

With the background of Made in China 2025 and Germany's Industry 4.0 strategy, combining the new generation of information technology and digital twin technology to realize the interconnection between the physical world and the digital virtual world is one of the core technologies that promote the flourishing of the manufacturing industry and make digital manufacturing possible.

Due to the high cost of industrial and service robots in reality, maintenance costs are high. In previous projects that we participated in, CloudMinds provided robots in Blender's digital twin design without considering motion compliance detection. When migrating the motion implemented in the digital twin environment to the motion of real CloudMinds Robots, if collision detection is not done to check if the migrated motion is compliant, this can cause damage to CloudMinds Robots, and then a high repair cost should be paid.

We reproduce the real CloudMinds Robots in Webots' digital twin at the same scale and manipulate the robotic arm to load and solve the collision problem, and provide timely feedback on the collision information and the rotation angle of the motor on the robot arm, as well as warning lights to remind the collision. It provides a solution to the digital twin design of CloudMinds Robots, and also a solution for industrial robots to be simulated and tested in the digital twin environment of Webots, which will greatly reduce the cost and subsequent maintenance cost.

© Springer Nature Switzerland AG 2022
R. Xu et al. (Eds.): ICCC 2021, LNCS 12992, pp. 44–51, 2022.
https://doi.org/10.1007/978-3-030-96419-1_5

## 2  Research Content

### 2.1  Webots Modeling

Webots kernel is based on the open source dynamic engine ODE and OpenGL based scene rendering [9]. This research proposal uses Webots instead of Blender and Unity 3D because Webots can perform collision detection and support the inclusion of various feedback components such as Touch Sensor and Position Sensor. Touch Sensor provides timely feedback on collision information and translates the collision feedback into whether to turn on the LED [1], while Position Sensor provides timely feedback on the motor rotation angle during collision. The left picture below is CloudMinds Robot in Blender simulation arm crossing scene. The right picture below is the same scale of CloudMinds Robot in Webots simulation of arm crossing scene. It is obvious that in the right picture, the left and right hands go through the model directly in Blender, while in the left picture, the left and right hands do not go through the model in Webots, and the collision information will be fed back in time [2].

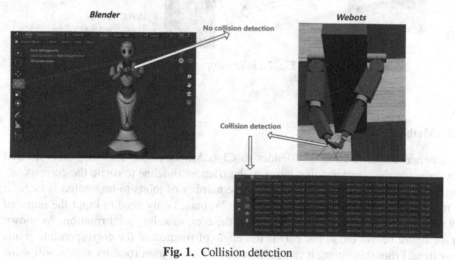

**Fig. 1.** Collision detection

Let's first explain the entire design architecture of the robot with a tree diagram. In the scene, we first create a Robot Node. We divide the child nodes of Robot Node [10]into three parts. One is the Body node, which is directly constructed by Shape. I choose to use the Box shape to represent the Body. The size of the Body is 0.0825 m * 0.34125 m * 0.06 m. The size is reduced in the same proportion by CloudMinds Robot, imitating CloudMinds Robot to a great extent. As shown in the figure below, I compare the robotic arm of Webots and CloudMinds Robot: set two degrees of freedom at the shoulder joint to ensure that the robotic arm can swing up and down and left and right. Two degrees of freedom are also set at the elbow joint, but the order of the two motors cannot be reversed [2]. The motor that rotates around the vertical axis is above the motor that swings from side to side. Because when the motor rotating around the vertical axis rotates 90°, the forearm can swing up and down instead of just left and right. If the motor sequence is reversed, this effect cannot be achieved; three degrees of freedom are set at the wrist joint (Fig. 2).

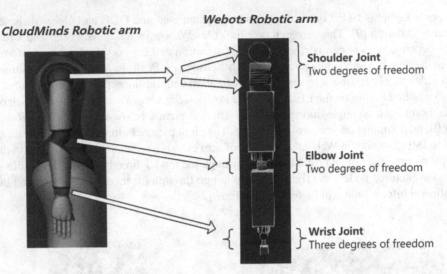

Fig. 2. Joint comparison

## 2.2 Method Comparison

To migrate human actions in Blender to CloudMinds Robot actions, I need to add keyframes to the corresponding joints in the Blender timeline to rotate the corresponding joints by the corresponding angle. If the number of joints to be rotated is large, it is tedious to add one frame by frame [3]. In Webots, I only need to input the required rotation arc through the program to realize the corresponding joint rotation. As shown in the figure below, the upper part is the angle of rotation of the corresponding joints over time. From this figure, it can be seen that different joint rotation angles will show different curves at each time point. The lower part is the rotating motor in Webots that rotates from one angle to another from its initial state. In Webots, the motor control is either position control or speed control [3]. In this research, I use Position to control the motor. In the program, I use the setPosition function to input the angle value to make the motor rotate the corresponding angle value (Fig. 3).

## 2.3 Angle Calculation from Coordinates

Below I demonstrate the process of transforming from coordinates to angle on a connecting rod model. As shown in the figure below, this model is a robotic arm lying down. Point A represents the shoulder joint, point B represents the elbow joint, $\alpha$ represents the rotation angle of motor_1, and $\beta$ represents the rotation angle of motor_2. Here I use forward kinematics, with the shoulder joint as the fixed point, motor_1 and motor_2

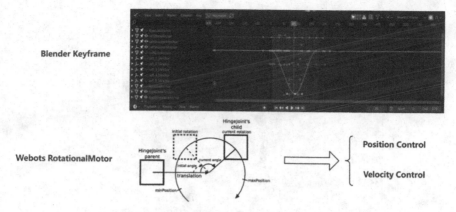

**Fig. 3.** Method comparison

rotate small angles respectively, and the look-up table continuously calculates the coordinates of the current elbow joint until it can rotate to the known coordinates of the elbow joint. First, I calculate the coordinates of point A based on α and β, and then calculate the coordinates of point B based on the coordinates of point A and the rotated α and β [3]. I use forward kinematics to create an index table of coordinates calculated from the angle, and keep looking up the table until I can find the corresponding coordinate point. The calculation formula is as follows (Fig. 4):

$$
A \begin{cases} x = L_1 \cdot cos\alpha \cdot sin\beta \\ y = L_1 \cdot cos\alpha \\ z = L_1 \cdot cos\alpha \cdot cos\beta \end{cases} \tag{1}
$$

$$
B \begin{cases} x = L_1 \cdot cos\alpha \cdot sin\beta + L_2 \cdot cos\alpha \cdot sin\beta \\ y = L_1 \cdot cos\alpha + L_2 \cdot cos\alpha \\ z = L_1 \cdot cos\alpha \cdot cos\beta + L_2 \cdot cos\alpha \cdot cos\beta \end{cases} \tag{2}
$$

## 3 Collision Detection

Crossing the arms of the CloudMinds Robot in Blender through Fig. 1 above directly cause the hand model to have a mold penetration problem, and there is no prompt for collision detection. On Webots, not only there will not be mold penetration, but there will also be a collision detection prompt. When transferring human motions to robot motions, because some joints of the robotic arm cannot rotate a large angle or do certain types of collisions (such as arms crossing, arms and body collisions), these actions will cause unpredictable damage to the robot [4]. Therefore, a series of designs for collision detection on Webots are as follows: In the digital twin design of CloudMinds Robot, there is a check mechanism for the field value of the rotation angle corresponding to the joint (Fig. 5).

And turning on selfCollision on the Robot node of Webots can effectively avoid internal robot collisions. However, for two Solids connected to each other through joints,

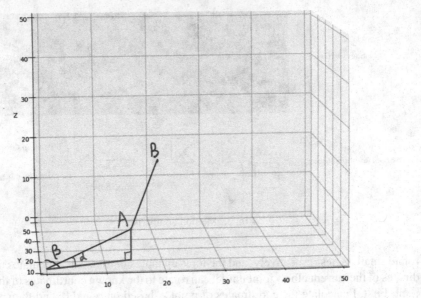

**Fig. 4.** Coordinates to angle

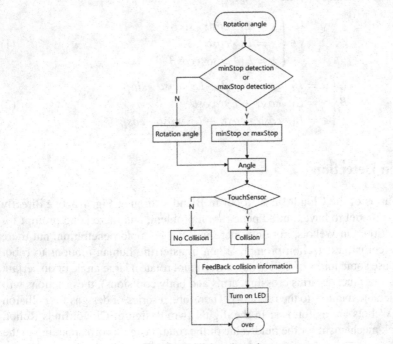

**Fig. 5.** Collision detection process

even if selfCollision is turned on, collision detection will not be performed. And a HingeJoint represents a joint and also represents a degree of freedom [4]. The robotic arm designed in this study has multiple degrees of freedom in the shoulder joint, elbow joint, and wrist joint. This will cause a HingeJoint and a Solid to be connected to each other through another HingeJoint. Even if selfCollision is turned on, collision detection will not be performed. For the above situation, I use the minStop and maxStop fields to solve the problem. First, give the motor a rotation angle, and it will check whether the value of this field is greater than maxStop or less than minStop. The minStop and maxStop fields define the hard limits of the joint. The hard limit is for the joint position, which is the physical (or mechanical) boundary that the motor cannot rotate to [5]. If the rotation angle value is within the specified range, then the rotation angle value is executed. Otherwise, the rotation minStop or maxStop value is executed. The corresponding joint minStop and maxStop field values are as shown in the figure below (Fig. 6).

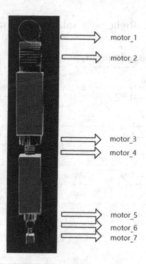

**Fig. 6.** Motor number

In the experiment, we collect the coordinates of the key points of the human body through OpenPose as shown in Fig. 7 a below, and calculate the angle of rotation of each joint using the above kinematic formula [6]. However, when the robotic arm is used to simulate the collision of the joints with other objects or other parts of the body during the rotation, as in Fig. 7 b below, we capture the collision of the left elbow with a human right hand, and the touch sensors will come into play [8]. I add touch sensors to each surface of the two solids of the robotic arm, each with LEDs on the surface. If it collides with a flat surface, the LEDs on that surface will light up. This not only gives feedback that the part has collided, but also alerts which plane has collided via the LEDs (Tables 1 and 2).

**Table 1.** Left motor rotation angle range.

| Joint | minStop(rad) | maxStop(rad) |
|---|---|---|
| Left_motor_1 | / | / |
| Left_motor_2 | −1.48 | 0.52 |
| Left_motor_3 | / | / |
| Left_motor_4 | −1.1 | 1.1 |
| Left_motor_5 | / | / |
| Left_motor_6 | −1.9 | 1.9 |
| Left_motor_7 | −1.6 | 1.6 |

**Table 2.** Right motor rotation angle range.

| Joint | minStop(rad) | maxStop(rad) |
|---|---|---|
| Right_motor_1 | / | / |
| Right _motor_2 | −0.52 | 1.48 |
| Right _motor_3 | / | / |
| Right _motor_4 | −1.1 | 1.1 |
| Right _motor_5 | / | / |
| Right _motor_6 | −1.9 | 1.9 |
| Right _motor_7 | −1.6 | 1.6 |

**a. Human action**

**b. Robotic action**

**Fig. 7.** Action migration

# 4 Conclusion

In the digital twin environment of CloudMinds Robot, there is no collision detection. When the human movement is transferred to the movement of the CloudMinds Robot, if collision detection is not performed, check whether the movement is compliant, which will cause damage to the CloudMinds robot. I have designed and modeled on the Webots open source platform. I use forward kinematics to solve the problem of calculating the angle from the coordinates [7], and controll the loading action of the robotic arm to solve the collision problem. Under the premise of not wearing the mold, the collision information and the rotation angle of the motor on the robot arm will be fed back in time, and there will also be warning lights to remind the collision.

**Acknowledgements.** This research has been supported by Shanghai Dianji University Research Foundation: (Grant No. G2-20-7201-003-05-045), Natural Science Foundation of China (Grant No. 62076160), Natural Science Foundation of Shanghai, China (Grant No. 21ZR1424700).

# References

1. Ji, Y.Z., Hou, L., Luo, L.: Combinatorial optimization algorithm-based inverse kinematics solution for 6R robot. China Mech. Eng. **32**(10), 1222–1232 (2021). https://doi.org/10.3969/j.issn.1004-132X.2021.10.011
2. Craig, J.J.: Introduction to robotics: mechanics and control. J. Automatica **23**(2), 263–264 (1987). https://doi.org/10.1016/0005-1098(87)90105-1
3. Brogardh, T.: Robot control overview: an industrial perspective. J. Model. Identi. Control. **30**(3), 170–174 (2009). https://doi.org/10.4173/mic.2009.3.7
4. Chen, Z.Z., Lin, L.M., Yan, G.Z.: MAS (Multi-Agent System) based multi-robot system: an important direction for the development of collaborative multi-robotics. J. Robot. **23**(4), 368–373 (2001). https://doi.org/10.3321/j.issn:1002-0446.2001.04.016
5. Thrun, S.: Probabilistic robotics. J. Commun. ACM. **45**(3), 52–57 (2005). https://doi.org/10.1145/504729.504754
6. Liu, H., Liu, D.Y., Jiang, Z.Z.: Review and prospect of space robotic arm technology. J. Aeronaut. **42**(1), 26–39 (2021). https://doi.org/10.7527/S1000-6893.2020.24164
7. Wei, Y.: Humanoid motion planning of anthropomorphic robotic arm based on action primitives. J. Eng. Sci. Technol. **53**(5), 183–190 (2021). https://doi.org/10.15961/j.jsuese.202000953
8. Lan, M.M., Wang, Y.M., Chen, X.X.: Research on humanoid robot simulation with Webots platform. J. Fujian Comput. **36**(5), 5–8 (2020). https://doi.org/10.16707/j.cnki.fjpc.2020.05.002
9. Xin, Y.X., Li, B., Hong, Z.: Modeling and motion control of a quadruped robot based on Webots simulation software. J. Qilu Univ. Technol. **30**(2), 45–51 (2016). https://doi.org/10.16442/j.cnki.qlgydxxb.2016.02.010
10. Han, X.G., Song, X.H., Yin, M.: 6R welding robot inverse solution algorithm and welding trajectory error analysis. J. Agric. Mach. **48**(8), 384–390 (2017). https://doi.org/10.6041/j.issn.1000-1298.2017.08.046

# Short Paper Track

# The WeChat Mini-program for Oral English Evaluation Based on the Smart Listening Algorithm

Ke Xi[1], Yufei Nie[1], Na Yang[2], Cheng Cai[1(✉)], and Aoxiang Zhang[1]

[1] School of Electronic Information Engineering, Shanghai Dianji University, Shanghai, China
caic@sdju.edu.cn
[2] School of Foreign Languages, Shanghai Dianji University, Shanghai, China

**Abstract.** This article introduces a WeChat mini-program for Smart Oral Evaluation. In this mini-program, we use Tencent Cloud's Smart Oral Evaluation interface and divide students into different levels, which can accurately return students' oral English scores and other details in real time. A typical feature of this algorithm is that it supports voice evaluation covering all ages from children to adults, with multiple modes such as words, sentences, paragraphs and free speech, by means of all-round scoring mechanisms including pronunciation accuracy, fluency, and completeness. The similarity of scores by experts is more than 95%, which can be widely used in oral teaching of Chinese and English. The mini-program based on the scoring algorithm of spoken language recognition solves the problem that the current oral English teaching under one instructor's guidance cannot be adjusted to the needs of every student in one class. After 70 days of experiments, it is proved that the oral English mini-program proposed in this article helps improve the oral English proficiency of each student.

**Keywords:** WeChat mini-program · Smart oral evaluation · Oral English

## 1 Introduction

With the wave of economic globalization, more and more countries are participating in the international division of labour. What follows is the interweaving and integration of diverse cultures and splendid ethnic groups [1]. From the perspective of youth education deployment and arrangements, English, as the most widely applicable language in the world, has received great attention and occupies a large proportion in China's education system. With the strong support of the 13th Five-Year Plan, the 14th Five-Year Plan and the reform and opening up policy, more and more companies from other countries have come to China for further development [3]. Therefore, for college students and corporate employees, oral English learning is very urgent and important.

Due to the current differences in the focus of education development in different regions, the oral English level of students, teachers, professional workers and company employees across the country is not consistent [2]. There are many problems to be solved in traditional oral English teaching. The summary is that most of the teaching is for large

R. Xu et al. (Eds.): ICCC 2021, LNCS 12992, pp. 55–62, 2022.
https://doi.org/10.1007/978-3-030-96419-1_6

classes, and it is difficult for all the students to talk to their content. Even if everyone has the opportunity to talk in class, their speaking time is rather limited. On the other hand, the practice and examination of oral English teaching are restricted by equipment and location. To be specific, teachers rarely have the equipment to effectively judge the self-generated oral English proficiency, and give students the timely feedback [4]. At present, considering the ever-increasing demand, the current educational resources that can effectively evaluate the oral proficiency are relatively limited. In traditional oral English teaching, the biggest problem is that for students at a higher level, what is taught in class is too simple and inadequate to improve themselves, and for students at a lower level, the in-class teaching is so difficult that they often find it hard to keep up with others.

The system introduced in this article is a learning environment oriented to oral English. For each student, our curriculum divides them into different levels according to their initial oral proficiency, and different levels have different oral practice contents, so as to conduct the layered teaching practice. Every week, the system will automatically update the level according to the student's performance of the current week. The higher the level, the more difficult the student's weekly test will be, otherwise, the less difficult it will be.. Therefore, this model will match the speaking difficulty to the speaking level of each student. Users can not only exercise and learn at their own level through the program, but also can quickly and intuitively see their own scores. Through the analysis of the scores, they can intuitively feel the changes brought to them by learning. At the same time, in the current era of online teaching, it is an online oral teaching platform. Users can effectively use the fragmented time to practice their spoken English.

## 2  Research Content

### 2.1  Speech Recognition Technology

In China, there are many API algorithm interfaces for oral assessment, and the most famous ones are Tencent Cloud's Smart Oral Evaluation and HKUST iFlytek [7]. We choose the Tencent Cloud's Smart Oral Evaluation for two reasons. One is that we are developing a WeChat mini-program. As this software development platform is owned by Tencent, it is more compatible in terms of adaptation. The other is that the parameters returned by Tencent Cloud's spoken language evaluation algorithm are more detailed with the following characteristics. The first is the coverage of all age groups. There are different scales of scoring mechanisms for students at different stages, and the evaluation results are quite professional and reliable. Second, the fine-grained evaluation provides multi-dimensional evaluation results concerning accuracy, completeness, light accent, pronunciation time, and degree of relevance. Third, its flexible access method can help novice developers get started quickly, and the interface is safe and reliable. These advantages help us to analyze the student's performance in the follow-up.

### 2.2  Principles of Smart Oral Evaluation

Based on speech recognition, the Smart Oral Evaluation will process the speech signals collected by hardware, and obtain the recognized text information and related evaluation scores after Subtract noise, feature extraction, construction of acoustic and language models, and pattern matching. It mainly includes the pre-processing stage, the model construction stage and the decoding stage. In the pre-processing stage, it mainly performs filtering, framing, available voice endpoint detection, feature extraction and other operations on the sound signals [8]. The feature extraction work converts the sound signal from the time domain to the frequency domain to provide a suitable feature vector for the acoustic model. In the acoustic model, the score of each feature vector on the acoustic feature is calculated according to the acoustic characteristics; the language model is based on linguistics-related theories to calculate the probability of the sound signal corresponding to the possible sequence of phrases; finally, according to the existing dictionary, the phrase is decoded to obtain the text information with the highest probability, which is then spliced and synthesized [9]. The scoring part combines the pre-processing information and the corresponding information of the recognized text, and performs further data analysis to obtain the fluency, completeness and accuracy scores. The Tencent Cloud's Smart Oral Evaluation has the following features. First of all, it is suitable for voice evaluation of users of all ages, adapted to the pronunciation characteristics of children and adults, and the evaluation results are professional and reliable. Secondly, the fine-grained evaluation provides multi-dimensional evaluation results such as accuracy, fluency, completeness, light accent, pronunciation time, and topicality, and the smallest possible phoneme-level correction capability as well [10] (Fig. 1 and Table 1).

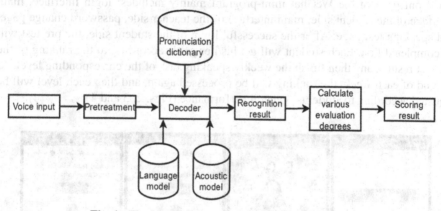

**Fig. 1.** The basic framework of Smart Oral Evaluation

## 2.3 Advantages of WeChat Mini-program

The main reason why we use the WeChat mini-program for development is that compared with native apps, a mini program has better adaptability [5]. It can avoid multiple model adaptations and the adaptation of the APP store by various manufacturers [6]. Besides, the mini-program development interface is simple, and we can observe the adaptation of different mobile phone models while the program is being developed. It comes with cloud development and cloud database, and its database is similar to mongodb. Using cloud development, our back-end management system can use the Tencent Cloud's CMS

**Table 1.** Data structure of Tencent Cloud's Smart Oral Evaluation

| Name | Type |
|---|---|
| SentenceId | Array of WordRsp |
| Words | Float |
| PronAccuracy | Float |
| PronFluency | Float |
| PronCompletion | Float |
| PronSuggestScore | Float |

management system. We do not need to spend a lot of time writing codes to have a fully functional back-end management system, which is convenient and efficient.

## 3 WeChat Mini-program

### 3.1 Front End and Design Backend Design

The front page of the WeChat mini-program mainly includes: login interface, main interface of the student side, main interface of the teacher side, password change page, and speaking test page. After the successful login of the student side, the pre-test will be completed first. Each student will get his/her grade according to the ranking of the pre-test results, and then finish the weekly speaking task of the corresponding level. At the end of each week, the ranking will be processed again, and then each level will be adjusted according to students' general performance (Figs. 2, 3 and 4).

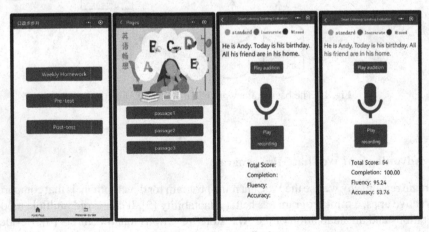

**Fig. 2.** Front pages display

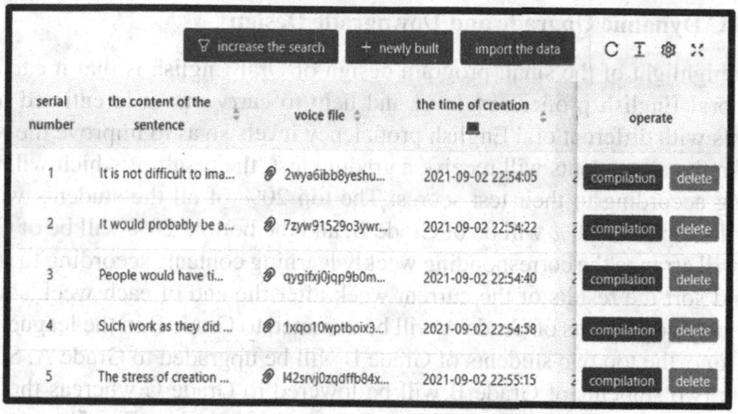

| serial number | the content of the sentence ⇕ | voice file ⇕ | the time of creation ⇕ | operate |
|---|---|---|---|---|
| 1 | It is not difficult to ima... | 🔗 2wya6ibb8yeshu... | 2021-09-02 22:54:05 | compilation  delete |
| 2 | It would probably be a... | 🔗 7zyw91529o3ywr... | 2021-09-02 22:54:22 | compilation  delete |
| 3 | People would have ti... | 🔗 qygifxj0jqp9b0m... | 2021-09-02 22:54:40 | compilation  delete |
| 4 | Such work as they did ... | 🔗 1xqo10wptboix3... | 2021-09-02 22:54:58 | compilation  delete |
| 5 | The stress of creation ... | 🔗 l42srvj0zqdffb84x... | 2021-09-02 22:55:15 | compilation  delete |

increase the search    + newly built    import the data    C I ⚙ ✕

**Fig. 3.** Content management system about passages

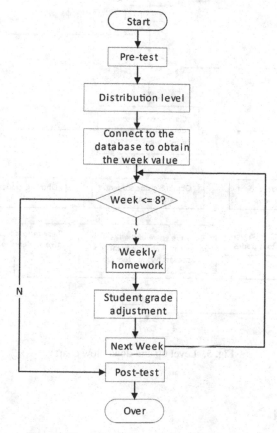

**Fig. 4.** The software flow chart of student side

## 3.2  A-B-C Dynamic Upgrade and Downgrade Design

The main highlight of the small program design of Oral English is that it can classify students' oral English proficiency level and help to carry out differentiated teaching for students with different oral English proficiency levels so as to improve the teaching quality. Firstly, all students will receive a grading test, the result of which will be used for ranking according to their test scores. The top 20% of all the students will be of Grade A, the top 21 to 80% will be of Grade B, and the bottom 20% will be of Grade C. Then we will arrange the corresponding weekly learning contents according to students' grades, and sort the results of the current week after the end of each week's learning. Later the last two students of Grade A will be demoted to Grade B in the league table; at the same time, the top two students of Grade B will be upgraded to Grade A. Similarly, the bottom two students of Grade B will be lowered to Grade C whereas the top two students of Grade C will be raised to Grade B in the league table (Fig. 5).

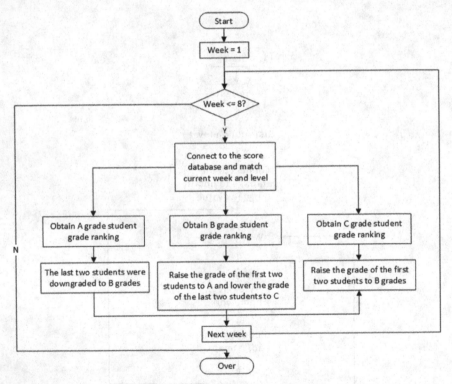

**Fig. 5.** Level up and down flow chart

## 4  Experiment

In the experiment, we invited 68 students to form the experimental group and 64 students to form the contrast group. Contrast group only takes the pre-test and post-test, whereas experimental group, in addition to the pre-test and post-test, also receives a 6-week training by using the mini-program. In this way, we can compare the experimental group's oral proficiency before and after the 6-week tests. Results prove that our oral English Mini-Program has a great effect on the improvement of students' oral English. The following two figures are the line chart of the experimental group after participating in the 6-week tests and the comparison histogram of the experimental group and the contrast group (Fig. 6).

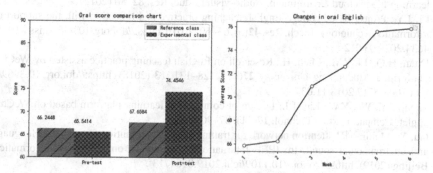

**Fig. 6.** Comparison chart of experimental results

From the first figure above, the oral proficiency of the experimental group was similar to that of the contrast group in the pre-test. But in the post-test, the performance of the experimental group was significantly better than that of the contrast group. The second chart shows that with the 6-week training via our mini-program, the oral English scores of the experimental group are getting higher and higher.

## 5    Conclusion

We rely on artificial intelligence voice evaluation to implement a WeChat mini-program. In terms of the algorithm credibility, after sampling and analysis, the sample audio is given to English teachers for evaluation and comparison. The collected spoken language index information has a high consistency with the manual evaluation. After the expert score is given, the analysis shows that the average score correlation between the voice evaluation system and the expert is 0.8, and the average score difference is 0.2. The result of the mini-program score is 95% similar to the expert score. This mini-program is compatible with Android, iOS and other models, which can meet all learners' needs. More importantly, we are based on Tencent Cloud's algorithm to solve the problem that the current oral teaching in schools cannot be adjusted to meet every student's needs in one class. With our mini-program, each student will receive different practice regarding their own oral proficiency.

**Acknowledgements.** This research has been supported by Shanghai Dianji University Research Foundation: (Grant No. G2-20-7201-003-05-045), Natural Science Foundation of China (Grant No. 62076160), Natural Science Foundation of Shanghai, China (Grant No. 21ZR1424700).

# References

1. Zhang, H.: Analysis of the practice of English teaching in the Central Plains cultural transmission under the background of "One Belt and One Road" construction. New Orient. English, 76 (2019). https://doi.org/10.3969/j.issn.1672-4186.2019.06.065
2. Tian, H.: Research on the construction and application of college English experimental teaching spoken language corpus. Overseas English (Part 1), 12–14 (2019)
3. Li, X.D., Zhang, H., Cao, H.H.: Research on oral English teaching model based on electronic learning file in cloud environment. Audio-visual Educ. Res. 82–86 (2013)
4. Li, J.Y.: Project-based college English teaching practice and reflection with the support of information technology. Teach. Res. **42**(3), 63–69 (2019). https://doi.org/10.3969/j.issn.1005-4634.2019.03.012
5. Duan, H.Q., Li, Y.M., Chen, H.: Research on English teaching practice assisted by WeChat platform. J. Mudanjiang University **27**(11), 128–131, 13 (2018). https://doi.org/10.3969/j.issn.1008-8717.2018.11.037
6. Shen, Z.Y., Wu, Y.W., Liu, J.J.: Design of competition learning platform based on WeChat applet. Comput. Knowl. Technol. **17**(21), 87–90 (2021)
7. Gu, Y.: Multimodal attention network for trauma activity recognition from spoken language and environmental sound. In: IEEE International Conference on Healthcare Informatics, Beijing (2019). https://doi.org/10.1109/ichi.2019.8904713
8. Li, X.G., Chen, S., Long, X.L.: A sentence-oriented automatic scoring method for oral Chinese-English translation. J. Chinese Inf. Process. **35**(7), 54–62 (2021). https://doi.org/10.3969/j.issn.1003-0077.2021.07.007
9. Ni, H.Q., Liu, X.M.: Design of a scoring system for spoken English pronunciation quality based on virtual reality. J. Sci. Normal Univ. **39**(11), 32–36 (2019). https://doi.org/10.3969/j.issn.1007-9831.2019.11.009
10. Liao, W.: Research on automatic assessment method of question-and-answer pronunciation for English learners. Guilin University of Electronic Technology (2014). https://doi.org/10.7666/d.D533402

# Constant Force Drawing of Chemical Fibers

Ruoyu Fang, Cheng Cai[✉], and Yuxiang Ren

School of Electronic Information Engineering, Shanghai Dianji University, Shanghai, China
caic@sdju.edu.cn

**Abstract.** Chemical fibers refer to fibers made from natural or synthetic polymer materials. In our daily clothing, such as T-shirts, high-end suits, socks and other knitted clothing, chemical fibers fabrics are widely used. Hence, their quality directly affects the quality of clothes. If the endurance and toughness of chemical fibers are not good enough, the clothes will wrinkle easily, which will in turn affect the look and quality of the clothes. For chemical fibers quality inspection, it is usually necessary to apply a constant force to the chemical fiber to ensure its quality. The traditional detection method is to hang the chemical fiber on a spring tensioner, but the spring and the chemical fiber have different physical properties, which will be extended over time, because the elasticity cannot accurately maintain a fixed tension. This paper proposes a method of constant force drawing of chemical fibers, which uses a screw slide table to apply tensile force. One end of the chemical fiber is suspended on the screw slide table, and the other end is hung with a corresponding weight. It employs Opencv, image processing technology, and orthography. In this experiment, using the camera to recognize the LED numbers of the electronic scale for weight feedback, the feedback of the weight value is used to adjust the movement of the lead screw slide table to achieve constant stretching of the chemical fiber.

**Keywords:** Chemical fibers · Constant force drawing of chemical fibers · LED numbers · Screw slide

## 1 Introduction

Chemical fibers are widely used in knitted clothing. If the quality of a chemical fiber is unqualified, it will cause wrinkles in clothing and affect its quality. Especially for some luxury knitted fabrics such as suits and dresses. If the chemical fiber breaks, it will cause wrinkles on the garment surface. For chemical fiber quality inspection, the best solution is to apply a constant force to the chemical fiber. The traditional method of using a spring tensioner cannot maintain a constant tension due to the elasticity of the spring and the chemical fiber itself. This paper proposes a method of pulling chemical fibers by using a screw slide table, hanging a weight with a fixed mass on one end of the chemical fiber, placing the weight on the electronic scale, using the camera to recognize the weight of the electronic scale at this time in real time, and feeding it back to the host computer. Considering the feedback quality, the upper computer controls the screw slide table to move up and down until the quality feedback of the electronic scale is at a fixed interval, and employs the method of controlling the constant force to pull the chemical fiber for quality inspection (Figs. 1 and 2).

© Springer Nature Switzerland AG 2022
R. Xu et al. (Eds.): ICCC 2021, LNCS 12992, pp. 63–71, 2022.
https://doi.org/10.1007/978-3-030-96419-1_7

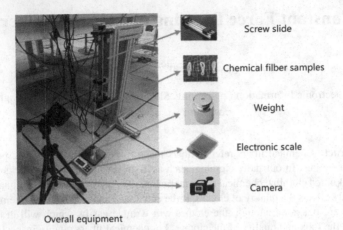

Overall equipment

**Fig. 1.** Experimental equipment and instruments

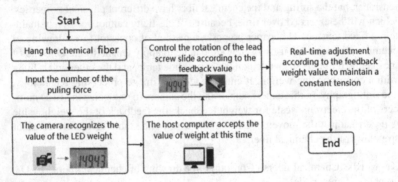

**Fig. 2.** Experimental process framework

## 2 Implementation

### 2.1 LED Digital Recognition

The method of judging how much force is applied to the chemical fiber requires real-time feedback of the weight. Initially, we used an I2C weight sensor to facilitate real-time feedback of weight information. However, in the actual measurement, the I2C weight sensor passes through the serial port, and the feedback quality value cannot achieve real-time feedback. In the quality feedback, there is a time deviation. As a result, the feedback value is not time-sensitive and cannot precisely control the rotation of the motor [5].

For the digital recognition of LED screens, we first adopted OCR text recognition, but the recognition rate of OCR for LED numbers is low, with the accuracy rate of about 60%, which cannot meet the requirements for weight accuracy.

We use a computer vision method to identify the number displayed on the electronic scale LED, and provide real-time feedback of the weight at the moment. The camera is used to recognize the captured digits of each frame of image and provide real-time feedback. The specific implementation is as follows.

First of all, in order to accurately locate the ROI area, which is the LED screen part, we use the Apriltag to locate the target. We put tags on the four corners of the LED electronic screen, and locate the area where the electronic scale LED screen is extracted. Using the method of orthographic projection, the target area is extracted (Fig. 3).

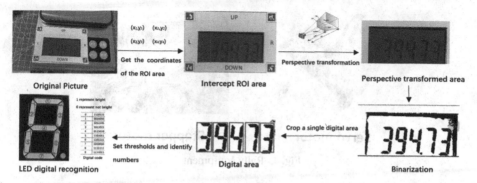

**Fig. 3.** LED digital recognition flow chart

The LED numbers have seven segments of transistors, and the brightness of each segment of transistors constitutes ten different numbers from 0–9. Then the intercepted ROI area is binarized, and each digital imaging area is intercepted [8]. Next the 7-segment transistors of each digital display are cut to determine whether each segment of the transistors is bright or not. We use 1 to represent bright, and 0 to represent not bright. The brightness of each segment of the transistor is judged according to the proportion of black and white of the image after binarization, and a certain threshold is set. If it exceeds a certain threshold, it is judged that the section of the picture tube is bright. Therefore, each number is composed of seven 0 or 1 code.

According to the code of each digital area, the current weight value is finally composed. We use the camera to capture the current weight value in real time. After testing, the algorithm for identifying LED numbers has the detection accuracy of 99.9% compared to the traditional OCR number recognition algorithm [9] (Table 1).

**Table 1.** Accuracy comparison

| Algorithm | Accuracy |
| --- | --- |
| OCR document recognition | 63.6% |
| Our algorithm | 99.9% |

## 2.2 Control of Screw Slide

After obtaining the real-time weight value feedback, it is necessary to control the movement of the motor to provide the pulling force to the chemical fiber. We have compared servo motors and stepper motors [1]. The rotation range of the servo motor is one revolution. When setting the minimum step length to adjust the tension, each time the minimum step is moved, the value of the weight fluctuates between 30 g–40 g, which does not meet the demand for constant tension on the chemical fiber (Fig. 4).

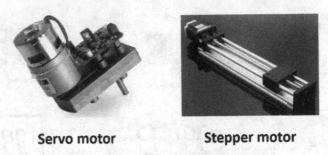

**Servo motor**          **Stepper motor**

**Fig. 4.** Rally equipment

Compared with the servo motor [4], the precision of the stepping motor of the lead screw sliding table is superior to that of the servo motor, because it does not accumulate errors, as long as the open loop control is performed, and the stepping motor generally does not lose steps. When we set the stepper motor to rotate with 6400 pulses per revolution, by setting the number of pulses, the tension value can be adjusted to drift around 0.5 g, which can meet our demand for constant tension.

Hang one end of the chemical fiber on the screw slide table, and hang a weight of a certain mass on the other end. For example, we need to provide a constant pulling force of 125 g, and we hang a weight of 500 fixed mass. When the weight feedback value of the electronic scale is 375 g, it means that the pulling force provided by the stepper motor is 125 g at this time. When the tensile force is stable at 125 g, due to the physical characteristics of the chemical fiber itself, it will extend over time. This will cause the tensile force to decrease. This requires real-time adjustment of the rotation of the stepping motor with regard to the quality feedback value. The chemical fiber is pulled up and down.

In order to make the stepper motor reach the designated position quickly, we set different pulse numbers at different weight feedback intervals to control the rotation of the stepper motor. We connect the Arduino to the stepper motor controller, using a common anode connection. We use DIR+ to control the moving direction of the stepper motor, and PUL+ to control the moving step length of the stepper motor [2]. We ese the host computer to send a serial port signal to the Arduino to control the up and down movement of the stepper motor and the step length of each movement, and set the Arduino pin to high and low output to realize the control of the up and down movement of the stepper motor (Fig. 5).

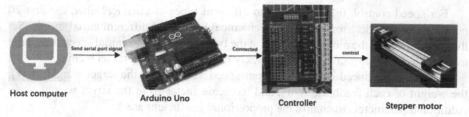

**Fig. 5.** Equipment wiring diagram

By pulling the chemical fiber at a certain initial speed, we can collect real-time feedback of different chemical fiber samples such as location, time, and weight. In order to increase the adaptability of the instrument to the stretching of different filaments, it is necessary to judge the filaments of different materials, whether it is a harder chemical fiber or a softer one. It is used to set the initial speed of the machine to prevent the chemical fiber from breaking and to reach the specified target weight quickly [3]. The machine feeds back data every 50 ms. Take the first 20 points and use the feedback value of the position and the current weight to calculate. We use the growth rate of the slope to determine the type of chemical fiber. The larger the growth rate of weight and position, the harder the chemical fiber, and the slower the initial speed setting. If the growth rate of weight and position is smaller, the chemical fiber is softer, and a faster initial speed should be set. The implementation is as follows:

First, we take the feedback values of the first and last points of the first twenty points, and set the weight feedback value of the first point as $W_1$, and the weight feedback value of the last point as $W_e$. Set the position feedback value of the first point as $P_1$ and the position feedback value of the last point as $P_e$.

$$rate = \frac{P_e - P_1}{W_e - W_1} \qquad (1)$$

According to the collected data samples, it can be found that for the softer chemical fiber samples, the weight of the first 20 points changes less with the position, while for the harder chemical fiber samples, the weight of the first 20 points changes more with the position. According to the collected data samples, it can be found that for the softer chemical fiber samples, the weight of the first 20 points changes less with the position, while for the harder chemical fiber samples, the weight of the first 20 points changes more with the position. Therefore, we set different initial speeds according to different chemical fiber samples according to the value of the rate.

For speed control, first, according to different types of chemical fiber, the first 20 points are used to determine the type of chemical fiber to set different initial speeds. Set the initial speed of the motor movement at the beginning, and the initial speed is as large as possible in order to save time and quickly reach the specified target weight.

Set the initial speed as $V_0$, the output speed value is $V_i$, the target weight as $W_t$, the weight of each feedback as $W_i$, and the scale factor from the target weight is $d_f$. Additional parameters to control the proportional coefficient are $\partial$.

$$d_f = \frac{W_t - W_i}{W_t} \tag{2}$$

The speed of each feedback output is $V_i$:

$$V_i = V_0 \times d_f \times \partial \tag{3}$$

Therefore, according to the above control algorithm, in a very short time, it can reach the designated target weight value. After reaching the designated target weight position, fine-tune the rotation of the motor to stabilize the weight value at the target weight value. Also set different initial speed values according to different chemical fiber samples. Adjust the speed of the motor according to the value of the weight offset, and the method is the same as the method mentioned above [6].

In order to prevent the chemical fiber samples with high elasticity coefficient from being too jittered during the adjustment process, set the difference between each feedback weight and the target weight as error. If the error increases, then decelerate. If the error has been decreasing, continue to adjust it according to the proportional control [7].

$$error_i = |W_t - W_i| \tag{4}$$

$$error_{i+1} = |W_t - W_{i+1}| \tag{5}$$

Calculate the difference between $error_i$ and $error_{i+1}$

$$rate = error_{i+1} - error_i \tag{6}$$

if rate > 0, set the speed to decelerate.

In the process of deceleration, according to the minimum controllable speed of the motor, it has been unable to reach the specified target weight. We calculate the cumulative error and set the minimum movement step size according to the feedback value of the cumulative error to make fine adjustments.

$$Error = \sum_i^n error\_\{i\} \tag{7}$$

If Error is greater than the set threshold, fine-tune the minimum step size. Through the above algorithm, by adjusting the speed of the motor, you can quickly reach the specified target weight and maintain a constant weight value.

## 3  Experimental Results

We have tested different types of chemical fibers with different elastic coefficients. In this experiment, 125 g, 200 g and 500 g tensile forces have been applied to three different types of chemical fibers. The experimental results are as follows (Fig. 6):

It can be seen from the above analysis diagram that for chemical fibers with different elastic coefficients and of different types, the method proposed in this article can quickly reach the specified tensile force value, and adjust it in real time in terms of the feedback weight value, and the final error can be controlled at about 0.5 g.

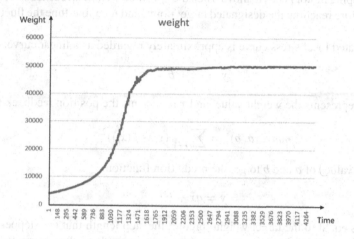

**Sample 500g**

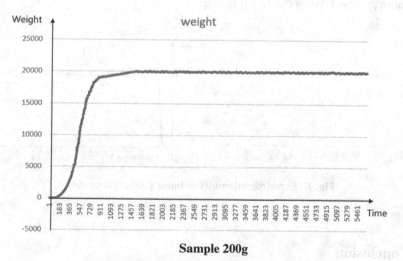

**Sample 200g**

**Fig. 6.** Experimental results of 200g and 500g

The above is to control the stepper motor by speed, and we try to use the position feedback mode to control the motor movement. The following is the realization of another control scheme.

We process the collected stress curve data. At the beginning, we make the stepper motor run at a full speed and get the weight and position feedback at the same time. We use 5 points in the value of each weight feedback to perform least squares fitting processing, and get the estimated stress curve. Due to the elastic coefficient of chemical fiber itself, the slope of the stress curve is increasing. When the slope has a large increase, 5 sample points are collected to form the stress estimation curve to predict the position where the stepping motor needs to move when the specified weight is reached. Decelerate in advance before reaching the designated target point, and then fine-tune the fluctuation of the weight.

The estimated local stress curve is approximately regarded as a linear curve:

$$y = ax + b \tag{8}$$

Where $y$ represents the weight value, and $x$ represents the position feedback value.

$$min\{L(a, b)\} = \sum_{i=1}^{N} (y_i - f(x_i))^2 \tag{9}$$

Solve the values of $a$ and $b$ to get the prediction function:

$$\hat{y} = a\hat{x} + b \tag{10}$$

When $y$ is equal to the target weight, predict the step length that the stepper motor needs to rotate, and decelerate to reach it stably. After reaching the designated target weight, the minimum step length of the stepping motor is used for real-time adjustment. The entire process takes about 15 s (Fig. 7).

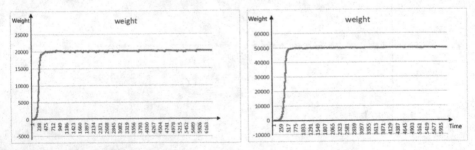

**Fig. 7.** Experimental results of linear prediction model

## 4 Conclusion

In this experiment, we used the lead screw slide table and electronic scale, and the Ardunio development board realized the solution of applying constant tension to the chemical fiber. An automated solution avoids applying constant tension to the chemical fiber to detect the quality of the chemical fiber. By identifying the LED numbers of the electronic scale, the real-time weight feedback value is obtained. The stepper motor moves according to the feedback value, and the maintenance of the constant tension is realized. The operator can input any tension value, avoid manual weight calibration, and achieve an error in the 0.5 g range [10].

**Acknowledgements.** This research has been supported by Shanghai Dianji University Research Foundation: (Grant No. G2-20-7201-003-05-045), Natural Science Foundation of China (Grant No. 62076160), Natural Science Foundation of Shanghai, China (Grant No. 21ZR1424700).

# References

1. Yuan, Y., Liu, W.: Design of PLC-controlled assembly robots. Electron. Test **2021**(21), 128–129–116 (2021). https://doi.org/10.16520/j.cnki.1000-8519.2021.21.045
2. Yuan, B., Chen, S.H., Wei, W.: Research on the development of a precision vegetable seeder based on stepper motor driven by the agricultural machine. **44**(07), 76–81 plus 87(2022). https://doi.org/10.13427/j.cnki.njyi.2022.07.013
3. Feng, M.Q., Zhu, W.B.: Constant force polishing method based on dynamic system and impedance control. Inf. Technol. **44**(08), 7–11 (2020). https://doi.org/10.13274/j.cnki.hdzj.2020.08.002
4. Braier, Z., Klouček, P.: System of measurement and evaluation of AC servo motor's mechanic, electric and control quantities. In: 2015 IEEE International Workshop of Electronics, Control, Measurement, Signals and their Application to Mechatronics (ECMSM), pp. 1–5 (2015). https://doi.org/10.1109/ECMSM.2015.7208691
5. Yang, S.Y., Fu, X.X., Wu, X.H., Xia, Q.: Tesseract-OCR's document scanning identification system. Electron. World (20), 98–100 (2021). https://doi.org/10.19353/j.cnki.dzsj.2021.20.042
6. Zhang, W., Yang, M.: Comparison of auto-tuning methods of PID controllers based on models and closed-loop data. In: Proceedings of the 33rd Chinese Control Conference, pp. 3661–3667 (2014). https://doi.org/10.1109/ChiCC.2014.6895548
7. Wang, S.Y., Shi, Y., Feng, Z.X.: Research on control methods based on fuzzy PID controllers. Mech. Sci. Technol. **30**(01), 166–172 (2011). https://doi.org/10.13433/j.cnki.1003-8728.2011.01.035
8. Wang, L.G., Zhang, Z.J., Li, J., Fan, Y.Y., Liu, L.Q.: LED light type font digital recognition based on convolutional neural networks. J. Electron. Measur. Instrum. **34**(11), 148–154 (2020). https://doi.org/10.13382/j.jemi.B2003005
9. Zhang, H.Y., Li, L., Zhao, J.B., Zhao, J.C., Tian, F.J.: Fuzzy PID-based force/bit hybrid control robot automated blade grinding processing. Combined machine tools and automated machining technology, pp. 147–150 plus 155 (2021). https://doi.org/10.13462/j.cnki.mmtamt.2021.11.035
10. Zhang, T., Wu, S.H., Cai, C.: Robot constant force control grinding method based on floating platform. J. Shanghai Jiaotong Univ. **54**(05), 515–523 (2020). https://doi.org/10.16183/j.cnki.jsjtu.2020.05.009

# Research on Multi-view 3D Reconstruction of Human Motion Based on OpenPose

Xuhui Li, Cheng Cai[✉], and Hengyi Zhou

School of Electronic Information Engineering, Shanghai Dianji University, Shanghai, China
caic@sdju.edu.cn

**Abstract.** With the development of the service robot industry, robot behaviors are more anthropomorphic, and human pose recognition has become an important research direction of machine vision. In the view of this situation, more research in the robot dance field is needed to solve the human-machine interaction, and promote the human-machine cooperative movement, the dance posture recognition and reconstruction in three-dimensional space. At the same time, the collected human actions are used as data for deep learning, so that the computer can learn the artificial solution strategies of the same problem, make more anthropomorphic actions, and solve practical problems on its own. Therefore, this paper proposes a motion capture scheme based on the multi-view recognition to record the posture by using the OpenPose models. It uses multi-view acquisition method to correct the acquisition errors caused by the perspective occlusion, and reconstruct people's dancing movements by calculating human key-points from different camera views.

**Keywords:** Machine vision · Human posture recognition · OpenPose · Multi-view vision · Apriltag

## 1  Introduction

With the continuous development of the robot industry in recent years, human-computer interaction scenes are frequently staged, and robots are increasingly anthropomorphic in behaviors. In the industrial field, the mechanical arm simulates the movement, grasp, handling and other actions of the human arm. In the service industry, robots play the role of reception and instruction [1]. With the expansion of the application field, more scenes of the human-computer interaction will appear [2, 3, 7].

Traditionally, sensors are used to measure the distance between the human body and the machine to create a three-dimensional space. In order to perceive an object, it may be necessary to calculate a large amount of sensor data, which calls for high requirements for computing power. In the field of robot dance, for showing the consistency of robot dance and the cooperation between robots, sensors cannot achieve the best performance. Therefore, the research direction of this study is focused on using machine vision to grab human postures through the multi-camera and calculating the position of each joint of human body [5, 6], and the repetition on the robots or visualization platform [9].

© Springer Nature Switzerland AG 2022
R. Xu et al. (Eds.): ICCC 2021, LNCS 12992, pp. 72–78, 2022.
https://doi.org/10.1007/978-3-030-96419-1_8

In this paper, the multi-view method is used to capture human dancing posture, and the Matlab and Apriltag are used to calculate the intrinsic and extrinsic parameters of the camera respectively so as to build the world coordinate system of the area. This research will use the OpenPose [12, 14, 15] to identify and estimate the human body posture, and the world coordinates of the human body key-points will be reconstructed in three dimensions, recorded in the JSON file and then reproduced with matplotlib.

The contribution of this research is to provide artificial solutions to practical problems for computers. Traditionally, programmers are required to design the operating trajectory according to the actual application scenarios of operating equipment such as robotic arms [4]. It requires a long preliminary preparation and a long development cycle. In this research, the human motion trajectory has been collected through multi-view cameras, and then put into the computer for deep learning, so that it can imitate the human movement strategy and make a motion trajectory that solves practical problems on its own, and has a more flexible application development scenario.

## 2    Detecting Materials and Method

### 2.1    Camera Calibration

In multi-view systems, a large amount of image information will be captured for processing calculations. In order to reconstruct the 3D scene according to the captured image, considering the impact of production and assembly and the data loss during imaging, we need to calibrate the camera and record the intrinsic and extrinsic parameter matrixes of the camera before obtaining the synchronous image frame. The coordinate system transformation in camera imaging is shown in Fig. 1.

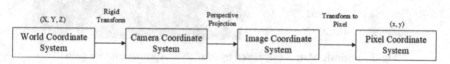

**Fig. 1.** Coordinate system transformation

When using two-dimensional coordinates to calculate three-dimensional coordinates, the formula (1) used is shown below:

$$\begin{bmatrix} X_w \\ Y_w \\ Z_w \\ 1 \end{bmatrix} = \begin{bmatrix} R & t \\ 0_3^T & 1 \end{bmatrix} \begin{bmatrix} X_w \\ Y_w \\ Z_w \\ 1 \end{bmatrix} = \begin{bmatrix} r_1 & r_2 & r_3 & t \end{bmatrix} \begin{bmatrix} X_w \\ Y_w \\ 0 \\ 1 \end{bmatrix} = \begin{bmatrix} r_1 & r_2 & t \end{bmatrix} \begin{bmatrix} X_i \\ Y_i \\ 1 \end{bmatrix} \quad (1)$$

Xw, Yw, and Zw represent the world coordinates of a physical point. After inversely multiplying the extrinsic parameter matrix, the camera coordinates of the point can be obtained for subsequent calculations.

## 2.2 Zhang's Calibration Method

When doing the calculation of intrinsic parameter matrix, Zhang's calibration method [16] is used to calibrate the camera in this research. This method is widely used in the field of computer vision because it does not require high-precision calibration objects, but only a printed flat checkerboard, to calculate the intrinsic and extrinsic parameters of the camera.

The checkerboard used by Zhang's calibration method has a large number of corners. After the checkerboard image is taken from different angles, abundant internal parameter information is obtained and the intrinsic parameter matrix is calculated.

By using the camera calibration tool in MATLAB, we can get the intrinsic parameter matrix of the camera. By temporarily ignoring the influence of extrinsic parameters, the intrinsic parameter matrix and the results are shown in the formula (2) and Fig. 2.

$$\begin{bmatrix} x \\ y \\ 1 \end{bmatrix} \sim \begin{bmatrix} f_x & s & x_0 \\ 0 & f_y & y_0 \\ 0 & 0 & 1 \end{bmatrix} [R|t] \begin{bmatrix} X \\ Y \\ Z \\ 1 \end{bmatrix} \qquad (2)$$

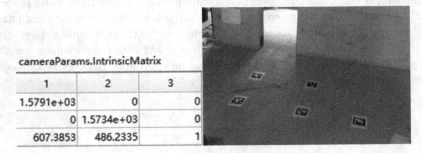

cameraParams.IntrinsicMatrix

| | 1 | 2 | 3 |
|---|---|---|---|
| | 1.5791e+03 | 0 | 0 |
| | 0 | 1.5734e+03 | 0 |
| | 607.3853 | 486.2335 | 1 |

**Fig. 2.** Intrinsic Matrix calculated by Matlab & Apriltag capture scene

In formula (2), $f_x$ is the focal length of the camera in the x direction, $f_y$ is the focal length value of the camera in the y direction, and $x_0$ and $y_0$ represent the offset generated by the image in pixels. Because there are five unknowns in the intrinsic parameter matrix, the values of intrinsic parameters can be calculated after collecting multiple groups of images, by using the least squares method to reduce the error value and improve the accuracy of the coordinate estimation.

Due to the development of lens technology, the distortion coefficients of most lenses on the market are very small. Therefore, only two radial distortions are considered in this study, which has a small effect on the error of the experimental results.

## 2.3 Apriltag

When using the Zhang's calibration method, there is also the calculation of the extrinsic parameter matrix. However, in this calibration method, the coordinate system is fixed on the checkerboard, and the application scenario is too narrow. Therefore, the method of pasting Apriltags is used in this study. The tag is arranged in the system, and the extrinsic parameter matrix of the actual camera position is calculated by using the obtained intrinsic parameter matrix through the position information of the identified key points. The scene is shown in Fig. 2.

## 2.4  Recognition and Acquisition of Human Actions

After capturing the synchronized frame images of the dancers, this study uses the Open-Pose to identify and estimate the joint point information of the human body. The Open-Pose is an open-source library based on convolutional neural networks, which can identify the postures of the body, face, and hands by setting the detector [8, 13]. At the same time, the pixel coordinates of each joint point are recorded in the image coordinate system to facilitate the subsequent calculation of the three-dimensional coordinates of the joint points and the reprojection of the joint points. This research uses the model of BODY_25 to recognize the structure of dancer's body. The picture of the model is shown in Fig. 3.

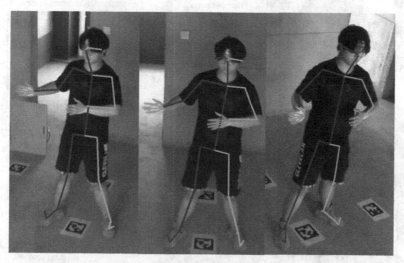

**Fig. 3.** OpenPose Model Body_25 & Recognition Results

When processing images, due to the angle limitation of the camera arrangement, the position information of each joint point of the body cannot be recognized completely. The traditional three-view method is to estimate the position of the joint point [4]. In this study, a multi-view solution is adopted, and the three-dimensional coordinates of the joint points are calculated from the visible perspective by capturing images from other views. Then use the score of the identified joint point to determine whether to discard the fuzzy point or the invisible point so as to use other views to supplement the pixel coordinate data required to calculate the joint point position.

## 2.5   Reconstruction

After obtaining the three-dimensional coordinates of each joint point, the dancer's dance movements can be reproduced in a virtual or real scene [10, 11]. In this study, the matplotlib package is used and the python reconstructed dance movements are used. When reproducing, due to the limitation of the view, the joint points of some frames are missing. Therefore, the limbs and hand postures are traversed outward from the easy-to-recognize human joints such as the root node (node.0,1,8) of the model.

# 3   Posture Recognition Results

## 3.1   3D Model Display

Considering the two radial distortions, the intrinsic parameter matrix obtained by Zhang's calibration method is shown in the figure, and the calculated pixel error is very small so as to influence the results. The pixel error in shown in Fig. 4.

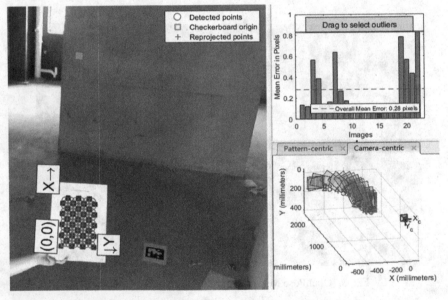

**Fig. 4.**   Chessboard Calibration & Projection Pixels Error

The human body posture recognized by the OpenPose in the dance movements collected from multiple views is shown in the following figures. It can be seen that the recognition error rate rises with the increase of the lens inclination until the joint points are not visible.

After obtaining the three-dimensional coordinates of each joint point, matplotlib is used to reproduce the dancer's dance movements, and can be subsequently loaded on the humanoid robot to realize the dance reproduction. The results are shown in Fig. 5.

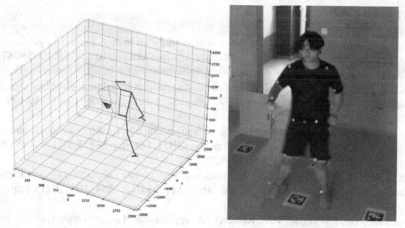

**Fig. 5.** Reconstruction Result & Errors of re-projection

## 3.2 Re-project to 2D Pixel Coordinate System

In this research, the physical world coordinates of the obtained three-dimensional model are re-projected back into the two-dimensional image by using the intrinsic and extrinsic parameter matrix of the camera. By comparison, the error pixels of each joint point in the X, Y direction can be calculated so as to know the accuracy of the model and the error of the wrong frame. The error in X direction is about 2.9301, and the error in Y direction is about 1.1904. The result image after re-projection is shown in Fig. 5.

## 4 Conclusion

When recognizing human postures and recording world coordinate information of human body key-points, sensors are a very accurate solution. However, in fast human-computer interaction scenarios, computer vision can also be used to obtain high-precision limb movements and human joint point movement information. In this study, the physical coordinate position of each joint point is still very accurate after multi-view supplementary calculation. It can reproduce the dancer's dance movements, which is great for performing specific functions in future application scenarios.

In the future human-computer interaction application scenarios, convenience, speed, and efficiency brought by computer vision will become a greater concern in human-computer interaction application technology.

**Acknowledgements.** This research has been supported by Shanghai Dianji University Research Foundation: (Grant No. G2-20-7201-003-05-045), Natural Science Foundation of China (Grant No. 62076160), Natural Science Foundation of Shanghai, China (Grant No. 21ZR1424700).

# References

1. Yang, J., Zhang, S.J., Zhang, C.H.: Comparative study on human action recognition based on OpenPose. Sens. Microsyst. **40**(1), 5–8 (2021). https://doi.org/10.13873/J.1000-9787(2021)01-0005-04

2. Fu, N.N., Liu, D.M., Cheng, X.T.: Fall detection algorithm based on lightweight OpenPose model. Sens. Microsyst. **40**(11), 131–134, 138 (2021). https://doi.org/10.13873/J.1000-9787(2021)11-0131-04

3. Guo, Y., Guo, C.X., Shi, X.: Research on human-machine adaptability of tables and chairs based on OpenPose learning sitting posture analysis. J. Forestry Eng. **5**(2), 179–185 (2020). https://doi.org/10.13360/j.issn.2096-1359.201909016

4. Tan, L.X., Lu, J.Q., Zhang, X.N.: Phantom machine gesture interaction system improved based on lightweight OpenPose. Comput. Eng. Appl. **57**(16), 159–166 (2021). https://doi.org/10.3778/j.issn.1002-8331.2004-0201

5. Zhu, H.K., Yin, J.W., Feng, W.Y.: Research and application of a lightweight real-time human pose detection model. J. Syst. Simul. **32**(11), 2155–2165 (2020). https://doi.org/10.16182/j.issn1004731x.joss.20-FZ0308

6. Duan, J.C., Liang, M.X., Wang, R.: Human body gesture recognition based on human bone point detection and multilayer perceptron. Electron. Measur. Technol. **43**(12), 168–172 (2020). https://doi.org/10.19651/j.cnki.emt.2004343

7. Tang, X.Y., Song, A.G.: Human body posture estimation and its application in rehabilitation training scene interaction. Chin. J. Sci. Instrum. **39**(11), 195–203 (2018). https://doi.org/10.19650/j.cnki.cjsi.J1803879

8. Liu, Y.C., Xu, S.C., Song, S.C.: Traditional Wushu action recognition and comparison based on OpenPose. Electron. Compon. Inf. Technol. **5**(3), 126–128 (2021). https://doi.org/10.19772/j.cnki.2096-4455.2021.3.058

9. Li, F.R.: Globally optimized multi-view stereo reconstruction system based on 3D laser scanning technology. Laser J. **42**(07), 75–78 (2021). https://doi.org/10.14016/j.cnki.jgzz.2021.07.075

10. Chen, J.T., Shi, S.D., Zheng, J.Q.: Head and shoulder posture estimation in sitting posture based on neural network. Sens. Microsyst. **40**(1), 9–12, 16 (2021). https://doi.org/10.13873/J.1000-9787(2021)01-0009-04

11. Chen, R.W., Yuan, T.T., Huang, W.B.: Application of convolutional neural network in driver attitude estimation. Opt. Precis. Eng. **29**(4), 813–821 (2021). https://doi.org/10.37188/OPE.20212904.0813

12. Cao, Z., Hidalgo, G., Simon, T.: OpenPose: realtime multi-person 2D pose estimation using part affinity fields. IEEE Trans. Patt. Anal. Mach. Intell. **43**(1), 172–186 (2021). https://doi.org/10.1109/TPAMI.2019.2929257

13. Simon, T., Joo, H., Matthews, I.: Hand keypoint detection in single images using multiview bootstrapping. In: IEEE Conference on Computer Vision and Pattern Recognition, pp. 4645–4653 (2017). https://doi.org/10.1109/CVPR.2017.494

14. Cao, Z., Simon, T., Wei, S.: Realtime multi-person 2D pose estimation using part affinity fields. In: IEEE Conference on Computer Vision and Pattern Recognition, pp. 1302–1310 (2017). https://doi.org/10.1109/CVPR.2017.143

15. Wei, S., Ramakrishna, V., Kanade, T.: Convolutional pose machines. In: IEEE Conference on Computer Vision and Pattern Recognition, pp. 4724–4732 (2016). https://doi.org/10.1109/CVPR.2016.511

16. Zhang, Z.: A flexible new technique for camera calibration. IEEE Trans. Patt. Anal. Mach. Intell. **22**(11), 1330–1334 (2000). https://doi.org/10.1109/34.888718

# Author Index

Printed in the United States
by Baker & Taylor Publisher Services

Printed in the United States
by Baker & Taylor Publisher Services